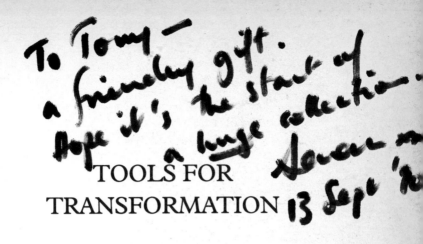

TOOLS FOR TRANSFORMATION

A personal study

by

Adam Curl

Dedication: *Tools for Transformation* is dedicated to
Isabel Cabot with love and gratitude.

HAWTHORN PRESS

Published by Hawthorn Press
Bankfield House, 13 Wallbridge, Stroud GL5 3JA, United Kingdom.

First Edition

Printed by Billings & Sons Ltd, Worcester.

The publication of *Tools for Transformation* was made possible by the generous assistance of the Rowntree Charitable Trust and many individuals.

Cover photograph credit to Oxfam, U.K.

British Library Cataloguing in Publication Data

Curle, Adam
Tools for transformation : a personal study.
(Social ecology series).
1. Society. Development.
I. Title   II. Series
301
ISBN 1 869 890 21 3

Contents

Foreword
by Elise Boulding

'Mediation'; 'development'; 'education'; what ordinary words to describe the task and tools of transformation Adam Curle is writing about! Don't be fooled. You, the reader, enter this book at your own risk. In his long journey from World War II soldier to college professor, adviser and mediator on the Indian subcontinent, in West and Southern Africa as well as in Europe and the United States, Adam's path has taken him through fields of blood and torture, lands dessicated by mindless economic planning and minds dessicated by false teaching. To read this book you must journey with him. There are no easy parts where you can rest.

Why should I say this is so hard? We have all read enough about the horrors of war, maldevelopment and bad schooling to be able to handle one more book about it. True, but we haven't been asked to love the bastards we read about. Whether we work in protest and social change movements or in the safer professional fields of peace studies and conflict resolution, we have learned to arm ourselves with righteous indignation about the malfeasance we continually observe. When you are travelling with Adam you can't do that, because you are with a mediator.

For Adam, the role of mediator is a transforming role both for himself and for those with whom he works. The stilling of the self so as not to impose personal reactions or carry loaded messages as he moves back and forth between two warring camps, the looking with the eyes of love at the divine core in bloody-handed generals, the listening to the other in ways that open channels from mind to mind and heart to heart so new words can get through, this is a mediation that goes beyond what the books tell us. It is a process intimately connected with development and education, all of which are tied together by creative listening.

Adam knows all the best of textbook mediation, and he has a sound theoretical understanding of the social systems and political, economic and cultural structures within which he must work. Working in the nongovernmental sphere, he documents little known aspects of citizens' diplomacy, carried out with no public fanfare. He also has credentials as a professor of education and psychology at prestigious universities on both sides of the Atlantic. As both a practitioner and one of the founders of the academic field of peace studies, he cannot be accused of fuzzy-mindedness or of preferring abstractions to reality. Yet his very sensitivity to the ugliest aspects of human behaviour has led him to look past the self-constructed misery of the human race to the underlying problem of undeveloped humanity.

As a Quaker and then a follower of the teachings of Tibetan Tantric Buddhism, Adam has come to look past the world's power struggles to the condition of individual human beings. We are ignorant of our true natures, says Adam. We fail to understand that all humanity is one, that we are irrevocably interdependent. By following the illusions of ego, in all its individual, corporate and nationalistic forms, we have been caught up in greed and in hatred for those who would deprive us of that for which we are greedy. In chasing illusions we are destroying ourselves and our world.

Adam is a visionary content with modest goals. He does not expect war-fighters to become peacemakers, economic planners to become Gandhians, teachers to become like Paolo Freire. He only hopes to whittle away a little bit of the illusory perceptions of reality to which they all cling. He wants to bring people a little bit closer to what is really there. He helps the entrapped to find small realistic steps that can be taken on the long road toward peaceful settlement of raging quarrels, or toward rebuilding abused local skills and resources, or toward a re-opening of minds closed by rote learning practices.

Adam speaks to a rage that is in all of us, a rage that wars wage unchecked because the belligerents reject negotiation as a sign of weakness, that starvation is widespread when food could be there for all, that all the resources put into education seem to extinguish the thirst for understanding. All of us who read this book will have worked in one way or another to assuage these evils. How can Adam be so sweeping in his assertions of the illusory nature of societies' perceptions of what is, so confident of the transforming power of mediation, development and education when rightly conceived, and so modest in his expectations of the outcomes of transformational activities?

I think it is because he is so intensely aware of the interconnectedness of all the elements in the system we know as life-on-earth. It does not matter where we start. Any mindful action undertaken in a spirit of love will help the transformative process along. It is not up to us to set the timetable, only to act with love. I said at the beginning that readers enter this book at their own risk. The risk is that you too will be called upon to re-examine your own illusions, to seek the reality behind the illusions, and to find a hitherto unsuspected part for yourself in the long slow work of transformation for humanity.

Acknowledgements

It makes me very happy to express warm gratitude to those who have been so generous with their help to me, both in writing this book and in the work and thought on which it is based. These include particularly His Holiness the Fourteenth Dalai Lama for teachings, empowerments and support, the late Lama Thubten Yeshe for his friendliness and lucid exposition of the Tantra, and Geshe Kelsang Gyatso for patient guidance.

I am also most grateful to many members of the Society of Friends (Quakers) and especially to the following for companionship and guidance, especially in mediation, in many parts of the world: the late Mike Yarrow (also for his splendid book referred to in the Bibliography), the late Walter Martin, Nicholas and the late Ruth Gillett, Joseph Elder, Joel McClellan, Trish Swift, N. Ramamurthy, and Roger Wilson who was my early mentor in both education and development, which are two main themes of this book. I should acknowledge here my privilege in being an heir to the three-centuries-long peace making tradition of the Quakers. I would not, however, wish to burden either them or the Society with any responsibility for what I have written; the views I have expressed and the conclusions I have drawn are a personal interpretation of what I have experienced, and the flaws and mistakes are all mine.

I owe deep thanks for the friendship of John Blacking, a musician and ethno-musicologist who also held chairs of anthropology, and for what I have learned from him of the universality of the great human qualities. To my grief he died while this book was in the press.

I also owe a great deal intellectually to a man whom I only met recently, and that briefly — Fridjof Capra. He showed the similarity between the worlds perceived by the oriental mystics and the contemporary physicists, thus giving a new meaning to the concept of reality; and, second, how the principle of inter-dependence, so central to physics (and of course Buddhism), could be transferred to economics, medicine, sociology and other disciplines still to a large extent stuck in the conceptual strait-jacket of Newton and Descartes.

Two members of my family have been wonderfully helpful and patient and I am deeply grateful to them: my wife Anne, who has read and corrected the manuscript and suffered more or less without complaint as what she calls a 'computer widow', and our daughter Deborah who typed part of the first draft and made superb use of her educational skills in teaching me how to use a word processor.

And there are many others, some completely unknown, some only slightly or through their writings, who have contributed to what I have been able to set down here: I realise very well that nothing I write is 'my' creation, it is merely a synthesis of countless influences that have played upon me during the course of this and other lives, and I am glad to acknowledge them. In particular I would like to thank many women friends to whom I owe what understanding I have of half the world. I regret that the enormous debt I owe them is not adequately reflected in the brief bibliography, but they have taught me so much more than books. And some have taught me with their books as well. Here I would single out, with gratitude and admiration, Elise Boulding and Joanna Macy who have also written most generous introductions to two of my books, Jo Vellacott, Alice Wiser, and Pam McAllister, whom I have never met but who for me symbolise the collective wisdom of women. I am also most grateful to Dr Marion Berghahn and to Berg Publishers Ltd., of which she is the creative founder, for permission to reproduce parts of my *In the Middle: Non-Official Mediation in Violent Situations*. These occur in 'Active Mediation' Parts I and II.

I should perhaps say something about the presentation of this book. I have resisted the academic temptation to garnish it with notes and references. The first reason for this is, that like many texts in my first discipline, anthropology, the author is the chief source of the material discussed. More important however, is the fact that this does not purport to be a scholarly work, but to suggest a particular approach to the *reality* of various human and social situations; I feel that following up academic hares would merely distract attention from this. Instead I have included a short bibliography of works that could supplement or amplify what I have written.

Introduction

We bring our miseries on ourselves and on each other. Even when the source of the suffering seems to be a purely natural calamity - the withering drought, the disastrous hurricane, the earthquake, the forest fire, the tidal wave, close scrutiny reveals a human factor. Apathy, indifference, inefficient use of existing resources, corruption, disorganisation, exploitation by the more powerful, and above all greed have changed what should have been a manageable emergency into a catastrophe. Even on the individual scale the anguish of those stricken by illness will vary greatly according to their attitude towards themselves and their affliction.

Like all who have reached my age and sadly many much younger, I have witnessed a vast amount of human unhappiness and am increasingly impressed by our responsibility in the fields with which I have been most concerned; I shall try to show how the problems involved can be tackled, at least in part, in the light of the human element.

I do not mean, of course, that the material issues of war, famine, poverty and so on must not also be dealt with on the relevant material and scientific levels of economics, agronomy and political action. We must also, however, adopt the right courses of action, the right attitudes towards ourselves and others, the right forms of behaviour to elicit co-operation and understanding instead of fear and confusion. In particular, we must encourage all concerned to *want to do the right things*. For example, it is useless just to berate the official who carries responsibility in a particular situation, for his inertia or incompetence. Instead, he should be helped to unravel the complexities he is trying to cope with, to identify what he might with advantage have done differently and then be given friendly help in so doing.

Unfortunately human error, and hence human suffering, is very common. We take it for granted that we shall do the wrong things and then pay the sadly heavy cost. Or even more often we think we are doing the right things and so slide with the best of intentions towards disaster. But it may be possible to change our perceptions and so counteract or avoid our errors.

Some forty years ago the now unrecognisable being who must for convenience be called 'I', emerged, with other survivors of his generation, from the shadow of war.

We then started, or tried to start, to resume our lives. In my case there was not much to resume. I had hitherto played at life. As an apprentice anthropologist I had been on a couple of expeditions, but I had explored the world and my reactions to it rather than the societies I was supposed to be studying. I had an amateurish interest in mysticism and Eastern religion, and had been instructed in the Gurdjieff system by his dissident pupil, Ouspensky, but not got very far. In addition I had had some extraordinary experiences with Sufi dervishes on one of my expeditions. In the months before I left the army, which had cocooned my mind for five years, I had luckily had the chance to learn enough psychology to obtain a few years later, a university post in the subject. I had experienced family life, as much as is possible without a fixed home and with only occasional short periods of leave, and had two children.

Fortunately I was able - things were much easier then than now - to get a good professional job (as staff member of the Tavistock Institute of Human Relations) as soon as I had left the university to which I had returned for a year to complete my degrees. I still felt something of an amateur (and do so, in fact, to this day), but was happy, confident and optimistic (and indeed still am). In this mood I made myself a promise that I have kept, although somewhat laxly, never to work at anything that was not worthwhile.

The I of the late 1980s does not remember clearly what the I of the late 1940s meant by worthwhile. The present I (what this pronoun implies will be considered later in the Appendix 'Who Am I?') means by it the effort to fulfil the human potential for wisdom and compassion, both in ourselves and others. I suspect the earlier I had a rather loose concept of human well-being based on Tavistock principles of improved interpersonal and group relations. (I don't want to imply that I now reject these principles, but that I have added to them.) In any case, whatever my commitment was, it has led me through four decades of most interesting and varied experience which I shall use in somewhat personal fashion to illustrate the three main themes I shall be discussing.

Peace Making and Mediation. I mean this in the very general sense of attempting to change violent, hostile, suspicious, lop-sided, or unproductive relationships into ones which were friendly, cooperative and constructive. I began by working on problems of returned prisoners of war whose experiences had estranged them from their own families and social background; then those of rural English communities that were in various ways alienated. (In fact I have discussed these in Part III which deals with one of the other themes, education; a fact showing how interwoven they all are.) Since the middle 1960s, however, I have been involved in the mediation of armed conflict in Asia, Africa and parts of Europe; this forms the basis of much that I shall have to say.

Social change. Specifically I have worked mostly on issues of what is often called under-development, the tragic concatenation of human miseries caused by poverty, especially in the southern hemisphere, and by the oppressive domestic and international policies usually associated with it.

Education. I mean this in three somewhat overlapping senses: the actual teaching of subjects (in my case social psychology and social science generally, including development theory, and peace and conflict theory); the principles of what makes for good or bad education - and what we mean by these terms; the relationship of education to social change and particularly to development. (Recently I calculated that my experience related to these themes included assignments, some long-term and some obviously very short, in over 40 countries of which over three quarters are in what is now generally called the Third World — I however prefer the term 'economically deprived countries' (EDCs) coined by my friend Walter Martin, which indicates that their straits can be attributed more to the depredations of the rich ones rather than to their own incompetence.)

These three spheres seem to me inextricably interconnected. The peace making I have been involved with has always been related to the sorts of political and economic factors that affect development; while equally the changes that come about as a result of development efforts, successful or unsuccessful, increase or decrease the likelihood of violence. Education, in the sense of the manner in which we evoke, discipline, cultivate, or distort the mind, is a vital element in everything that happens; it is an essential element — not scholastically but in promoting understanding — in both peace making and effective development work. All in all, it can be the precision tool for 'leading out' our most subtle and valuable potentialities. But it is well to remember also what Stalin said: 'Education is a weapon; everything depends on who wields it and whom it strikes down'.

Certainly these three activities have been closely and practically interconnected in my own life. My first international peace making assignment was to do with the Indo-Pakistan war of 1965; I had been development adviser on social affairs to the government of Pakistan between 1956 and 1959, and subsequently consultant on education for several months in 1963 and 1964. My involvement with the Nigerian civil war (the Biafran war) grew from earlier educational associations in West Africa and the fact that I had some measure of responsibility for an experimental school in Nigeria. For five years I was director of the Center for Studies in Education and Development at Harvard University, which knit together two of my main concerns in a single job. In the 1980s I was assessor (which basically means adviser) to the University of the South Pacific based mainly on Fiji, on education; there I was predominantly concerned with exploring ways in which education could promote development while also helping to preserve much valued traditional culture. These are examples taken at random from my experience.

I am sure that wise peace making, development work and education support each other in the maintenance of a just and harmonious society. Conversely, where the system is oppressive or corrupt it is hard for liberal education to exist or, of course, for the poor to prosper, while violence is seldom far below the surface.

I am naturally not suggesting that these things are the sole or even the most important components of societies or nations. Together with political structure, the economy, the legal system, social traditions and many other elements they constitute structures of interacting and interlocking parts. Every human society, great or small, is so formed. Education, development and peace making simply happen to be the three parts with which I have been implicated. They represent, I believe, three types of force which exist in all circumstances and which, if constructive order is to be preserved, must be rightly related to each other. They are crucial tools for social transformation.

Development, in the sense of purposeful growth and change, represents what Gurdjieff would have called the active force; peace making, in the sense that it may act to restore a previously existing state of equilibrium, would be the passive force; education, being less an operative impulse than a source of knowledge and attitude that can help both development and peace making, is the neutralising force, a catalyst rather than an independent factor. But it is well to remember that the roles can switch; development may become the passive force if it serves chiefly to maintain or restore prosperity to the status quo; peace making may become active if the aim is to establish a new synthesis; education may become active or passive depending on whether it serves a progressive or a reactionary society. And so on.

I believe for these reasons that in discussing these three types of activity, I am taking ones which are representative in function of most important elements in society, even if different in detail from some of them.

My vaguely mystical streak, as is usual, did not survive my early adulthood. I moved into the stage of life during which we tend to face outwards rather than inwards. Young adults are apt to be concerned with getting the pattern of their lives clear, setting up a home and family, completing their training, getting established in work or profession, paying off the mortgage, educating their children, building up the ego of a conventionally successful human being.

During this period, which in my case lasted from approximately the early thirties (its onset probably delayed by the war — army life prolongs adolescence) until I was approaching 50. At that age I was still busy with my career which, after its late start, was going well. I had a chair at Harvard, was a fellow of the right learned societies, got invited to posh international conferences and to sit on important committees, had a nice home and a happy family: what else could anyone want?

But having fulfilled my professional ambitions, the whole

academic circus began to pall. I started to refuse invitations unless they offered to pay my wife's expenses as well. I was ready for a change of gear.

Then, in the middle or late 1960s, something extraordinary began to happen. According to a rash of recent books, most people remember with derision, retrospective horror, or occasional nostalgia, two chief things about this period. First was the neo-Marxist student revolt which nearly overthrew the French government and created havoc in the British, European and above all the American universities. The second was the 'permissive society', particularly the sexual revolution facilitated by the pill. But this is a very limited view.

When we first came to America, the students were respectful, wore ties, and called me 'sir'. The main controversy aired in the university paper, *The Crimson*, concerned parietals; this word, I discovered, meant the period during which a student of one sex could visit one of the other in his or her room. They then had to leave, if I remember rightly, at some absurdly early hour like 7.30 pm. The students advocating change argued passionately that it should be extended until, say, 8 pm. The professors, for their part, paternally concerned for the welfare of the students, explained with kindly gravity why this concession would undermine the whole structure of university life.

Then one day, the students suddenly threw away their suits and ties, put on jeans and called me Adam. The young women moved in with the young men and vice versa, staying not just till 8 pm, but all night. Even more significant, they argued that they should have a say, since they were at the receiving end of it, in academic policy.

But the core of the matter was even more important than demonstrating for equality: *the young had come to perceive a different reality*. They had ceased to see themselves through the eyes of their elders and teachers, almost as a different species, empty vessels to be filled with the wisdom, which they now saw as flawed, of the adult world. The claimed the right to choose how they lived their lives and how and what they were taught.

My initial reaction combined sympathy with irritation at these pretensions. They might *feel*, I thought, that they should have some influence in academic matters, but surely they must realise in their more sober moments that they were simply not qualified to make important decisions about their studies?

But gradually the revolution took hold in my own consciousness. I then suddenly woke up and saw that most of the students, certainly my very mature post-graduates, were just as capable of sound educational judgements — they knew perfectly well which teachers were good, or bad, and why; and what was claptrap and what was genuine — as their self-confident professors; but the latter, of course, felt threatened by any diminution of their authority. (I shall later discuss how this affected my own practice of education.)

The shift in perception extended much further that that, however. It covered, for example, the relations of the rich countries to the EDCs. I began to understand (and here returned Peace Corps volunteers were passionately illuminating) that we, the aid donors and workers — the 'experts' such as myself — had in general done the wrong things. We had foisted our inappropriate economic, agricultural, industrial and technological assumptions and bags of tricks onto these countries with disastrous results. Our 'generosity' had cost *them,* rather than *us,* enormous amounts of their scanty capital. Our development procedures, by chance, ignorance or, as I increasingly saw, by design, had been of greater advantage to the donor than the recipient - indeed, to the *dis*advantage of the unfortunate recipient. Coming to this realisation changed my outlook on development as radically as it had been changed on education.

Increased insight into my own racism and sexism equally altered my relations with American Blacks and other minority groups with whom I had close dealings, and with women. The last, and most significant evolution in awareness did not, however, mature for a couple of years. It came about like this.

From 1967 to 1970 I was involved as a mediator in the Nigerian civil war, a horrific struggle that absorbed most of my psychic energy. Early in 1970, with my wife and young daughter, I was in London for a period of sabbatical leave, and my journeys to Africa were made from there. One morning I had a telephone call from Arnold Smith, then Secretary General of the Commonwealth, with whom we had had close contact over the conflict. He told me he had just had news that indicated that the war, which had been expected to drag on for some months, was coming to a sudden end. Every one feared that it would finish, as it had begun, with atrocious massacres. Smith urged me to leave at once for the war zone. He thought that since I was fairly well known to the leadership on both sides, I might be able to do something to prevent the anticipated disaster.

I went as soon as I could, full of apprehension. I felt I must go, but had no idea what I could do when I arrived. I had an absurd fantasy of standing between the embattled armies like a traffic policeman, trying vainly to halt two lines of troops advancing implacably towards each other blazing away and ignoring my raised hands, and crushing me as they came.

But it turned out quite differently from how everyone had expected. When I arrived the war was already over. There was no massacre. On the contrary, the federal soldiers had done everything possible to help their rebel fellow-citizens — gave them their own food and money, took them to hospitals or feeding centres in their trucks, showed reconciliatory friendship in every way. The Biafran leaders (minus Ojukwu, their head, who had escaped to Ivory Coast) who had come to Lagos to sign the cease fire were not, as I had imagined they would be, languishing fettered in a dungeon. They were free to come and go as they pleased and one of them was even in the same hotel as me, strolling around and greeting old friends who had been separated from him by three years of war.

There was nothing for me to do. I stayed on for a few more days to tie up some personal loose ends of my work, and returned to London. I did nothing outwardly interesting during this period, but inwardly I was in a state of bliss. Obviously I was delighted at what had happened, but I also felt as though I had personally passed through a long period of testing and was now receiving the prize. While in this state it came to me with great clarity that I must now concentrate on my inner life; it was now time for my new awareness to spread from the political and psychological to the spiritual sphere.

And high time, too. I was then 53 and my inner life had lain fallow for years. It is true that my wife Anne and I had joined the

Society of Friends (Quakers) in Ghana a decade earlier, and this association was and has remained a valued source of support and purpose, indeed much of my peace work has been carried out under Quaker auspices. However, I felt the need for more inner guidance than Quakerism, probably through my own fault, had given me; I now set out to look for it. The path I followed led me through several stages, each illuminating, to Vajrayana, the Tantric Buddhism of Tibet. This might be called a philosophical psychology, or a psychological philosophy; it is a way of life rather than a religion with all the implications of dogmatic beliefs and an anthropomorphic supreme being.

I should emphasise that my attraction to this form of Buddhism did not imply that for me the teachings of the Buddha superseded those of Jesus or indeed of the Hindu and Sufi teachers I valued. But I must admit that I feel almost all forms of institutionalised Christianity (except for a few groups such as the Quakers) and of Islam, and indeed of some of Theravada Buddhism, to be agents of perversion.They have corrupted our understanding of reality and our sense of the divine; they have set us murderously against each other, reviling and even putting to death as blasphemers and heretics, the mystics and visionaries who upheld the truth beyond the official dogma; and the secular religions of communism and fascism have followed suit. But the teachings of the perennial philosophy express a universal vision shared by great spirits of every faith.

The reason for my involvement with Tibetan Buddhism is not, then, that I have discovered a new religion, but that I have found one which appeals to me particularly for the way in which it presents this philosophy. I am especially drawn by the constantly reiterated emphasis on kindness and generosity to all creatures; by the stress that enlightenment (salvation in Christian terms) should not be sought for personal spiritual gain but because it enables us better to help others; by the all-pervading sense of the unity yet ever-changing character of life; by the emphasis on non-violence, and on the essential goodness and interdependence of every being in the world; by the debunking of the ego, which I had long sensed to be the greatest — though or perhaps because illusory — enemy to human reason and happiness; by the rejection of the concept of sin, especially original sin, in favour of ignorance leading not to evil, but to 'unskillful' behaviour; by cheerfulness and fundamental optimism undimmed by clear sighted recognition of pain and disaster.

I was particularly attracted by the combination of the profound philosophy underlying the characteristics I have just mentioned, with the psychological method — the yogas, meditations and other practices. Through these the wisdom becomes not merely an intellectual grasp, but something that changes our perception of reality and in the process transforms our nature. In the following pages it will become clear that my work and my understanding of what have done in the past have been much influenced by what I have learned from the Tibetans, which provides a kind of framework for much that I shall be writing about.

(Having said this, however, and having expressed my profound debt to Quakerism, I should admit that I have never felt able to feel totally committed to any tradition or institution, religious, psychological or philosophical. I am a grateful guest, deeply appreciative of the wise help and warm hospitality I have received, but not a permanent resident — perhaps because I feel the house itself is essentially impermanent.)

In the quest for inner order that led me to this point, I was following belatedly in the steps of many others who saw that the underlying source of their dissatisfaction was a dim feeling that there was another truth than the conventional, one to be sought less in books than inward exploration. Hence an explosion of interest in Zen, yoga, Sufism, alchemy, pentecostal Christianity, Jungian and Reichian psychotherapy, Gestalt and, understandably but tragically, the heightened awareness conferred briefly by drugs.

Some of the 1960s students were carried along on a mindless wave of excitement, but there were many who had seen things differently, or who felt that there was another vision of the truth which they must seek. It is literal to stress *seeing,* for one of the inspirations of the period was Aldous Huxley's *The Doors of Perception.* In this he described how his vision of ordinary things was profoundly affected by mescalin; it is also metaphorically true in the sense that without the aid of drugs our understanding expands — we know things to be other than how we had previously understood them. For example, while earlier we may have claimed to *believe* that in some abstract or ideal fashion humanity is one, we actually *felt* that we were all isolated and separate beings. But now we may *know* that we are in a very real sense one, joined inseparably to each other, waves which are both part of each other and of the sea from which they arise and in which they are merged.

I understood also that a by-product of this search for reality was the questioning of conventional beliefs about — as I have already mentioned — such things as sex, race and development. I knew that some of our values were unsound and our interpretations faulty, but it had only been a half-awakening. A more complete (certainly not full) awakening began to come as I started to see that things such as certain moral precepts not only seemed unsatisfactory or undesirable, but that in any case they could be valid only in relation to particular circumstances; in attributing to them some ultimate truth I had largely misunderstood the fundamental nature of almost everything.

A comparison may clarify what I mean by this perhaps mysterious or pretentious statement. Newtonian physics gave a brilliantly reasonable and comprehensive model of the material universe. Although it has now been superseded so far as cosmology and sub-atomic physics are concerned by the new physics originated by Einstein and Planck, it is still valid in many practical spheres; but no one looks to Newton for any vision of the ultimate nature of the universe or the structure of matter.

So also in the realm of human affairs are two realities. One is the conventional reality of you and me, separate beings having their own names, family history, career, characteristics, appearance, etc. These are all facts we have to be concerned with if we are to live in this world. But underlying or transcending this, is another reality: that our separation is illusory; that we are ripples in an indivisible ocean; that we are bundles of undifferentiated energy in an incessant state of interaction in which we are completely *inter*dependent and indeed can be said to exist only in relation to each other. Thus for me a new sense of reality began slowly but radically to transform my mind. I saw that the illusion of *in*dependent existence was the source of enormous human suffering.

I don't, however, mean to suggest that we should refer to the conventional reality as materialistic, or to the ultimate reality as by contrast spiritual. Such words, especially if used to express values, are misleading. 'Spiritual' suggests that there is a separate realm of fine, sensitive, insubstantial essence to be contrasted with one of coarse, crude matter. This is a duality that offends the truth Whoever thought of galaxies or atomic particles as being either spiritual or material, or by the same token as good or bad? It is only necessary for us to try to understand all realities: to see them in right relation to each other is to come close to enlightenment, but to see only part of the truth is to live lopsidedly. Above all, I came to feel that our quest must be empirical. I no longer had any faith in a religion that expected us to believe in untested doctrines: the dictum *'credo quia impossibile'*, 'I believe because it is impossible', is not only contradictory, it is close to blasphemy, an insult to the truth. Almost the last words of the Buddha were an adjuration that his followers should find things out for themselves: 'be your own light'.

As my perception of my work has become less dim (though it still wavers and flickers) I have come to see that the way we perceive human nature, *especially our own,* is of overrarching importance. It is indeed an absurd illusion to consider that we can work for peace, which means to be actively involved with people who are behaving in an unpeaceful way, if we are inwardly turbulent and ill-at-ease; or to help people change their lives for the better if our own existence is disordered and impoverished; or to educate if our own human potential has not been sufficiently led out.

I also came to understand with increasing clarity the workings of what the Buddhists call the three poisons. These are: the conventional ignorance of the reality of our nature, craving or greed for what we feel will compensate for the consequent loss of happiness and stability, and hatred or fear of whatever interferes with that compensation. These in constant interaction are responsible for most of our personal miseries; on the institutional level they constitute the motive force for greedy and/or aggressive social and economic structures.

In the following pages I have tried to show two things. Firstly, how our planetary affairs have inexorably suffered because of our failure to respond to a vision of reality of which we are all intuitively to some extent aware because we are part of it, and which is expressed in all wise teachings. For me, as I have said, it is most systematically enshrined in Tibetan Buddhism, but the further I follow that path, the more I realise how much I owe to other faiths and realms of knowledge, including contemporary depth psychology and modern physics. I am surprised at the Buddhist flavour of some of my earlier writings before I encountered Buddhism, but all paths that are paved with reality rather than illusion converge at the same point. Once we are below (or is it above?) the superficial levels of consciousness, the personal and cultural begin to fade and we all see the same truths.

Secondly and principally, I hope to show how we might act, as I have falteringly attempted, in accordance with that vision of reality.

In Part I the principles for action derived from it are applied to peace making, in particular to the problems of mediation in large-scale violent conflicts.

In Part II we move on to issues of even greater enormity than stopping wars; preventing them from happening in the first place. This, I take it, is the ultimate goal of development, because violence breeds an atmosphere fetid with resentment, jealousy, suspicion, injustice, inequality, hatred and fear — all of which undermine not only peace but development in the more conventional economic sense (with which, in fact, this Part begins). In this Part I go beyond the personal experiences on which the rest of the book is based, to consider some infinitely larger questions of the global ordering of human society. This sounds pretentious, but at this perilous juncture we must, if life is to survive, have some goal for the evolution of civilisation . At the moment we do little but stagger from one emergency to another, one desperate piece of first-aid to the next. Unless we can act within the context of a wider purpose, a more comprehensive plan to lead us out of the sequence of disasters, then the next terrible crisis may be the last one.

In Part III education is discussed as the means of evoking the wisdom without which none of our problems can be solved.

These themes are drawn together briefly in the Conclusion. Those who may wish to examine more closely the relationship between the principles of the Vajrayana Buddhism of Tibet and what I have suggested concerning mediation, development and education, may like to read the Appendix in which some aspects of the Tibetan Buddhism are more fully, but still most superficially, examined.

Finally, this book is about the ways in which we may try to forestall the most catastrophic effects of human error and deluded ignorance. If that is impossible, as is clearly the case with wars already raging, we may learn to minimise them through mediation and so avoid some of the suffering to which they might have led. In either case we can only succeed by paying constant attention to the deeper truths of human nature, and the ways in which they may be realised.

PART I
Peace Making/Mediation

Chapter One
Introduction

When we are at war, there is general agreement on the meaning of peace: it is the end of the war. At other times, however, it is not so clear cut. The no-war definition begins to break down in those places where, although there is little or no overt violence, there are political oppression, economic exploitation, detention camps, arbitrary arrest and imprisonment without trial, persecution of minorities, and other loathsome practices. Surely only a regime that condones such abuses could claim that a state of peace exists.

We also speak of peace in a much more personal or subjective way; we feel at peace, we have peace of mind, the atmosphere, we say, is peaceful. But there is not necessarily any association between inner and outer peace; we can feel peaceful in a violent setting, or unpeaceful in a tranquil one.

Because of these ambiguities I have found it more practical to speak of peaceful and unpeaceful *relations*. I use this term because whatever the context, the peaceful — or unpeacefulness is normally *between* units, whether they are nations, groups or individuals. Even in the case of a single individual, peacefulness probably results from harmony between the various parts of his or her make up (perhaps right and left brain, or as the Tibetans would believe, male and female elements), while the unpeacefulness reflects their discord or separation.

A peaceful relationship I would characterise as one on the whole doing the participants more good than harm. On the small scale of a man and woman this would mean that in general, though no doubt with occasional lapses, they give each other support, comfort and love, and create a happy home for their children. In an unpeaceful relationship, they make each other (or one makes the other) uneasy, guilt-ridden, lacking in confidence, resentful, bad-tempered, while their home would be unpleasant to visit. Even more fundamentally, doing good to a person is helping her or him to realise their potential for wisdom and compassion; doing harm is to impede this realisation.

On the international scale, a peaceful relationship between one or more countries would be characterised by close diplomatic ties, frequent exchanges of political, cultural and educational visits, minimal restrictions on commerce and, above all, sufficient mutual trust and understanding to resolve without friction any differences that might arise. An unpeaceful relationship would obviously imply the lack of these things and therefore the possibility in cases of dispute of resort to the ultimate arbitrament of war.

When I refer to a peaceful relationship doing more good than harm to those involved, and an unpeaceful one more harm than good, the terms have connotations that differ with the context. On the individual level these are more psychological and sociological; at the larger, or international, level, more political, economic and military.

There is, however, a common thread. Ultimately what determine the quality of a relationship are the reactions, the personal responses however much influenced by externals, of individual women and men. Whether they are ordinary citizens or heads of state, they are equally capable of manifesting the great quality of wise compassion — and the insidious venom of the three poisons of ignorance, hatred and greed. The former impels us to sensible and humane actions. The latter impairs our capacity for transformation, we remain stuck in a morass of pain and confusion into which we draw others; the mind is clouded with negative emotions that weaken awareness and smother kindness and generosity. In addition, the poisons create conditions, national and international as well as familial — rising to the extremes of physical violence, persecution and famine — in which the struggle for sheer survival virtually precludes, for most, the quest for the ultimate reality.

The task for would-be peace makers must be on two levels. They must dig out the roots of unpeacefulness within themselves; the blindness, the illusory sense of 'I', the cravings and antipathies and guilts. Without this effort, however partially successful, they can never hope to have any real effect on others.

They must also, on the external level, work against the institutions that derive from and in turn stimulate the three poisons — the divisive class systems, the rapacious economic structures, the repressive regimes, the insane war machines. But the outer is also the inner level because institutions can only be influenced through the human beings involved with them. And our contact with these is inextricably linked to our contact with, our awareness of, our own nature.

Working for peace, then, is working for the transformation of the world. Is this foolishly arrogant and boastful? No, provided we think coolly, remembering that everything we do, say, or think does have a universal impact (albeit one we may never be able to identify). Although it would be absurd to consider that we shall ourselves effect a great change, every moment of our lives can either contribute to the *trans*formation or the world, or to the *de*formation being wreaked upon it by the three poisons. In this context, to do *no*thing is to do *some*thing, and quite possibly the worst thing. So act we must, and if we do so reasonably and intelligently we may hope to serve the ultimate goal.

What I have just written would suggest that before discussing mediation, development and education as differing but complementary routes towards the same goal, I should talk about self-transformation as part of the process. I do not, however, feel qualified to do this; in this sphere I am very much a learner rather than a teacher. I can only say that I try to realise, that is to make real within myself experientially, the precepts and principles set out (mainly in the Introduction and the part of the Appendix called 'Who Am I?'); and that I do this through pondering and meditating, and the practices taught me by kindly masters under whom I have studied and at times lived with throughout my life.

Chapter Two
Mediation

One great obstacle to the transformation of the world is the mass violence of war, perhaps the ultimate product and expression of the three poisons. It is not only serious for the obvious reasons of the suffering caused and the danger to the whole global system; when wars abound — there are about thirty raging as I write — the inter*dependence* of this system is thrown out of gear; the inter*action* of course persists, but it is baneful rather than constructive — consider the dangerous and disruptive repercussions of Vietnam, Afghanistan, the Gulf, or Southern Africa. In addition, however, war exemplifies and so may tend to exacerbate the most destructive illusions of the ego — anger, hatred, despair, guilt and the sense of separation, and the mindless cruelty and acceptance of violence that comes to infect whole communities.

The purpose of mediation is to abate these illusions in the men and women who are charged with fateful decisions in times of crisis. To the extent that this is achieved, they may be better able to make realistic efforts to end the conflict by negotiation. Mediation, it should be stressed, is not negotiation, which has to do with argument, bargaining and compromises between protagonists trying together to find their way towards a settlement. Mediation is a *psychological* effort to change perceptions both of the conflict and of the enemy to the extent that both protagonists gain some hope of a reasonable resolution and so are more prepared to negotiate seriously. In this way it might also be thought of as an indirect assault on the three poisons.

I shall try to describe what this means, both in practical terms of what mediators actually do and of the principles that affect their attitudes — which of course affect what they do.

First, I should say that the term mediation means different things to different people. To some it means the work of a Henry Kissinger or George Schultz shuttling between capitals and doing what would sometimes be more accurately described as diplomatic arm twisting. To some it means the courageous solo effort of Terry

Waite, though this to my mind would be better described as advocacy or special pleading for the unfortunate hostages, of which as I now write he is one. To some who have little to do with international affairs, it is marriage guidance, industrial conciliation, the efforts of community workers to bring together mutually hostile factions, the arrangement of reparation by criminals to their victims. In some cases it is, or is thought to be, a brief process of a few days or at most weeks (I thought of my own first experience in this way). What most of these ideas of mediation have in common is exemplified by the title of a short book of mine on the subject; *In the Middle*. Mediation is carried out by people who are in the middle of a quarrel in two senses; they both stand between the parties who are antagonistic to each other, and they are perforce in the centre of the activities that not only arise from but also create the antagonism.

It is this that all forms of mediation have in common. What they also have in common is the human element. In the last resort mediation is about men and women, the attitudes that make for conflict between them and the attitudes that make for peace.

What differs apart from the context — domestic, industrial, community, international, etc, is the approach of the mediators. They may think of their work as largely psychological (marriage guidance), diplomatic and political (international disputes), managerial (industrial), and so on.

Their status also differs. The marriage guidance counsellor or the promoter of reparation tends to be something of an authority figure, a professional on the par with a doctor or lawyer. The same is true, or more so, with some international mediators who hold or have held high office, such as the UN secretary general or former US president Jimmy Carter. Such eminent figures in the international sphere are usually so busy that they have to exert their considerable influence over a fairly short span of time.

The mediators with whom I have associated have had a somewhat different status and modus operandi. They have mostly been members of the Society of Friends working with Quaker support and loose direction from Friends House in London or the American Friends Service Committee in Philadelphia (though about a quarter of my work has been done more or less on my own). Since Quakers, like Buddhists, believe in the essential goodness of human nature and in the futility of violence as a means of resolving human conflict, their approaches to peace making would seem to have much in common. I write somewhat inferentially as there is, so far as I know, little Buddhist literature on the subject though what I have heard directly from the Dalai Lama would seem to confirm this.

It seems to me that over the last two or three decades many Quaker mediators have adopted a particular approach to and style in their work. I would not, however, wish to imply that this is the only or the best way. Its main characteristics are that it combines psychology with diplomacy and that it tends to last a long time, probably years rather than months.

It is largely psychological, although its overt arguments may be mainly political or strategic,because it aims to alter the way in which the protagonists view themselves, each other and the conflict. Our experience shows that wars may drag on because each combatant has so distorted a perception of the other's character that a non-military resolution seems impossible. The attempt to bring about a change in understanding will include continual interpretations of what the other side is saying, explanations of their attitudes, exposure of false rumours, therapeutic listening, and the development of a personal relationship of trust and friendship with decision makers on both sides. By such means tensions of hostility and anxiety may be reduced to a point where cautious hope prevails.

The diplomatic character of the mediation does not consist of pressuring or persuasion. These would imply that the mediators were trying to promote their own solution to the conflict, and were perhaps doing so at another's instigation. To do so might possibly be permissible to forestall an otherwise unavoidable catastrophe, but it would be a dangerous precedent to abandon the key principle of even-handedness. The diplomatic work of mediators can be described as active mediation (described later in some detail) which tries to eradicate the misconceptions and the exaggerated fears and suspicions that prevent opponents in conflict from coming together to resolve their differences; it is not an effort by mediators to do this for them.

The psychological and diplomatic aspects of mediation are of course closely interwoven and depend for their effect on the degree of confidence both protagonists have in the mediators themselves.

The long duration of most mediation is due to the complex and desperate aetiology of most wars; it would be unreasonable to suppose that they can be settled quickly, except by some non-mediatory force which merely suppresses the symptoms of violence temporarily without removing the causes. Mediators are ultimately concerned with changing the habits of mind that generate and sustain these causes (though of course they will seize any chance of alleviating the symptoms and thereby perhaps contributing to a final settlement). All this takes time. It may also take time to establish the relationships with key decision makers who are in a position to make fateful choices regarding the war.

Another characteristic of international mediation as I know it, is that it is private in two senses of the word. Firstly, it is not being carried out on behalf of any organisation, such a government, which may have a particular stake in the type of resolution achieved. If otherwise, the protagonists will probably view mediators with a certain wariness. However much they may be liked and trusted as individuals, everyone understands that in the last resort they must serve the best interest of their paymasters and that these may conflict with those of the people who are fighting the war. To this extent they will be treated with reserve. This may even be the case with mediators sent out by a neutral international body such as the United Nations or the Commonwealth, which might be (and in my experience have been) disliked by one or other of the protagonists.

This mediation is also private in the sense that those involved receive no payment, except for travel, hotel and other necessary but not lavish expenses. When this is understood mediators are usually recognised as being motivated by purely humanitarian considerations and therefore probably trustworthy. But it is also true that this private, non-official status has certain disadvantages. Mediators usually have to make their own travel arrangements and hotel bookings and to do such tiresome chores as sending cables (which in some places may take a whole morning), wrestle with the local authorities over visas and other permits, and hire cars or even on occasion, charter planes. This can be an added burden to the inevitable strain of mediation in tense and difficult circumstances. The mediators' local embassy or consulate may indeed by very helpful in supplying information of many sorts, but it is vital to avoid relying on it too much, certainly not to the extent of getting material help such as transportation. In the suspicious atmosphere of war, this might well suggest partisan mediation or even that it was a cover for espionage of some sort.

I might conclude this section by saying that I have been engaged in this sort of mediation over the last twenty five years and considerably longer in different though analogous non-violent circumstances. During about two third of this time I have been involved in one or other of five major mediation efforts (and from time to time minor ones). I do not mean that I was in the field the whole time, but when I was not and was getting on with my normal life as husband, father and university teacher, the problems of violence and reconciliation were continually on the back burner of my consciousness and my bags were packed, metaphorically and often literally, for a return to the front at short notice.

Chapter Three
Fundamental Mediation

In this brief pause between the more abstract discussion of mediation as an especially psychological aspect of peace making and its more practical aspects, I would like to outline what might perhaps be called a yoga of mediation. This term may sound phoney or fanciful. It is, however, meant in the more precise sense of a spiritual/psychological discipline, something that joins together inner and outer events. The first element in the situation is the mediator(s) in whom the common illusions of 'I', or the ego, are heightened by working under stress, often far from home, in conditions of confusion and violence. S/he is likely to suffer anxiety verging at times on considerable fear, an acute sense of loneliness and separation from whatever was relied on for emotional (and indeed physical) security, the temptation to think harshly and judgementally about the 'bad' qualities and stupidities of those involved in the conflict, and alternating feelings of powerlessness and omnipotence. These stand in the way of both wise appraisal of the situation and genuine rapport (which is only possible when the 'I' is stilled) with leaders in the struggle.

The second element consists of those leaders. At the outward level of relative reality, they obviously have a great deal to cope with. By every mundane objective standard, they are beset by all possible types of danger and difficulty, economic, political and, obviously, military. But their 'I's, like those of mediators, are put under particular sorts of strain by the circumstances of violence. They too feel loneliness and isolation, as I shall explain later in detail. They tend to have exaggerated illusions of power and omniscience to counterbalance the hidden fear of failure and defeat; when things go wrong there is sometimes a violent oscillation of mood between despair (carefully concealed) and manic overconfidence. The 'I' expands, to identify itself with the nation, guerrilla band or whatever is involved; when the larger group is in jeopardy, so is the ego of the leader. Such are the sources of the paranoid fears and suspicions so often noted in war-time commanders. All these reactions militate against the detachment and realism required for a sensible view of the existing situation and of course the possibilities of fruitful negotiation.

Mediators must, obviously, try to cope with their own disabilities as well as they can. If they are to be at all effective in their peacemaking role they must also act in a way that reduces the destructive force of ego-based and generated illusions in those with whom they are talking. A large part of this task is obviously to speak with them and to act in a way which will allay fear, anger and suspicion. They must also speak in a manner that is calm, sensible and friendly; they must show consistent and genuine good will, this can not be faked for long and mediators must strive to deal with feelings of dislike, fear or repulsion. This is of outstanding importance. They must be especially careful that they say and do nothing that threatens the ego of leaders, causing 'loss of face'. They must constantly attempt to communicate with their — the leaders' — real, their ultimate identity. This is perhaps often done better by serious *listening* rather than by speech, except the spontaneous speech that comes from this listening. Consciously planned efforts to address someone's 'better nature' or soul or however we think of it, are seldom successful.

(I have not mentioned what might be considered by some as the conventional diplomatic skills based on knowledge of the current political and military situation, acquaintance with key people and understanding of the requirements of protocol. I assume that all mediators in the international or governmental field have this necessary background. What they may lack is an idea of the more subtle context in which these basic skills and understandings must be exercised if genuine progress towards reconciliation is to be made.)

Chapter Four
The Atmosphere Of Violence

In this section I shall mainly be considering how leaders, in the sense of officials — heads of state or leaders of armed factions, prime and other ministers, high civil servants and military commanders (and others entitled to make decisions affecting the course of a war) — react to the violent situation.

Some of what I shall say may seem derogatory. I should therefore make it clear that most of the forty or so leaders I have personally dealt with were decent and well-motivated women and men. Their response to crisis has, in general, been courageous, resolute and conscientious. If it has also sometimes been obstinate, intolerant, proud and vengeful I would still not wish to blame the individuals concerned; the pressure on the fallible self, the 'I', is for them considerably greater than most of us are called upon to bear.

It must be realised that the position of these leaders is extremely difficult; the more the responsibility, the more the strain, both physical and emotional. Some, not perhaps without grounds, are in constant fear of assassination.One whom I knew to be both cool and courageous, General Yakubu Gowon, Head of State of Federal Nigeria during the civil war, felt constrained to remain almost continuously in his army headquarters guarded by soldiers of his own tribe, the Angas of the Middle Belt of Northern Nigeria. And apart from murder there is often the fear of a coup engineered by the opposition (if there is one) or dissidents in the ruling group. A tense and watchful atmosphere of almost universal mistrust may easily develop. Leaders may ask themselves whether their aides and other officials are telling the truth. There may be no one on whom they feel they can rely; some officials may conceal the facts because they do not want to cause distress, thus a drab military picture is misleadingly brightened by reports of success; others may try to curry favour by exaggerating the efficiency of their ministry or military command; yet others try to suppress evidence of their ineptitude or corruption. Who is to be trusted? Anxious suspicion thus becomes a regular habit of mind.

For these reasons mediators, once they are to some extent accepted and liked, may develop a function beyond straightforward (if it ever really is) mediation. They become in some measure friends of the leaders with whom they are dealing. I am not suggesting that they actually become intimates — they usually lack a sufficient background of culture or position. However because they are consistent in their good will and attempted helpfulness, and because they are completely outside all local factions or traditional rivalries, leaders may feel it is possible to relax with them and in some measure to confide in them. Befriending, in fact, is a significant function of mediators. It may, indeed, lead to a somewhat strange intimacy. On one occasion, I received an intimation that an attempt might be made on the life of the president of a country in which we were trying to mediate. I also gathered that he might be safer if he remained in his office and that if I were with him, my somewhat unexpected presence might serve as a deterrent. The attempt was, it seemed, to be made on the day after my return from a temporary absence. As soon as I got back, therefore, I told him what I had heard. 'All right', he said. 'We will spend the day together'. So we did. At one stage he had to keep an appointment elsewhere, so we sallied out in what he assured me was a bullet-proof car — to my relief, however, this quality was not put to the test. When we got back it was dark and we felt any danger was past. He thanked me and sent me to my hotel with an armed guard (most unQuakerly) in the bullet-proof car.

The atmosphere of conflict may seem hard, tough and pragmatic and so in one sense it is; the conduct of the campaigns is planned with ruthlessness and precision. But when we consider the underlying layer of motives, apprehensions and — often — ideology, we enter a realm of chaotic emotional unreason. War engenders a mental environment of desperation in which fear, resentment, jealousy and rage predominate. The 'I' is menaced and mobilises to resist threat. In addition, as I have already noted, the 'I' of leaders tends to become almost inseparably identified with the idea (in fact, their idea) of a national or group identity. Nations do not have the consciousness to possess any sort of identity; this is not what Jung meant by collective unconscious. Nevertheless, people often impute a strong psychic identity, with which they associate themselves, to their country. Our thoughts about our country and ourselves become to some extent fused — and confused; both we and our country are dogged John Bull, wise and stern, but benevolent Uncle Sam, or beautiful and passionate Marianne; in this way we — and still more so our leaders — may become deeply identified with the victories or defeats of our country, its international reputation, its glories and shames. Our own hang-ups and inner conflicts become entangled with our feelings for our nation and its predicaments. Hence, as has been remarked, the onset of hostilities is often marked by a surge of unreason in which fantasy and reality become inextricably intertwined. Truth, it has been said, is the first casualty of war.

A related phenomenon is that we displace the guilt from which we all suffer in some degree, onto the enemy. In the case of leaders, the guilt we commonly feel for the inadequacy of our lives, the repressed conflicts of infancy and veiled fear that we are denying the truth of our being, is supplemented by a more rational guilt for the misery and slaughter they are causing. For them to accept all this as 'my fault' would be too much for the already sensitive 'I' to bear. But luckily it can be legitimately projected outwards onto the foe: it is he who is to blame. They only did, and reluctantly, what was necessary to defend *their* innocent people from *his* brutal and unjustified aggression.

One of the dominant emotions of embattled leaders is suspicion. It takes little to change their modicum of cautious uncertainty into paranoia. This all too often impels them to take action that appears to justify their suspicions. Take, for example, the American dread of communism. For decades this has caused successions of presidents to support oppressive tyrants as bulwarks of democracy and to help them in their efforts to crush liberal opposition. Not surprisingly these oppositions often found that their only source of help was in communist countries. How right we were, say the pundits of the Pentagon as they engage in a crusade against men and women fighting, as their own ancestors had done two hundred years ago, a war of independence.

The mirror image is a typical feature of violent situations. I experienced it fairly early on in my mediation work.

I was shown in to meet the leader of one of two embattled states. He was most cordial and after a few minutes of polite chit-chat he said: 'I'm glad you have come to see us, because you will now learn the truth about this terrible affair which has been so misrepresented in your press. We are even portrayed as the aggressors! In fact, as I am sure you have discovered already, we are only fighting to defend ourselves from the ruthless aggression of our enemies. We would agree to any reasonable terms if we could only believe that they would come to the conference table with the slightest intention of serious negotiation. But sadly enough the difference between us is that they are brutal and violent and only want to destroy us, whereas we are a peace-loving people, as all the world should know. I am happy to have this chance of warning you before you meet them not to be taken in by their lies; remember the atrocities they have committed and tell the world the truth when you return home'.

A short while later I met this man's opposite number and listened to an almost identical speech. He began by saying that he was glad I had come to see him because I would now learn the correct version of this terrible war which he regretted so bitterly, being absolutely dedicated to the cause of peace. But after the utterly unscrupulous and unprovoked attack by his enemies, who were little better than wild animals, he had no option .... and so on until he reached his peroration about telling the world the truth when I got back.

I then commented mildly, if somewhat unkindly, that it was strange, but what he had just been saying about X was almost the same as what X had said about him. (I was reminded of Tweedledum and Tweedledee.)

He was amazed. 'But that's absurd', he said. 'Everyone knows that we are a peace-loving people whom those devils attacked without the slightest provocation .... etc. ...etc.'

This might all sound ridiculous and hypocritical if it were not for the fact that both men genuinely believed most of what they were saying. This too would sound absurd did we not know how perceptions are distorted in other situations of stress and anger. I have several times spoken separately to members of estranged couples about their break-up. It was hard to imagine that the circumstances each one described had actually been the same, or that the decent if unhappy individuals I was talking to were the monuments of cruelty and insensitivity, or demanding and irrational bitchiness they described each other as being. But this was how they really saw each other and the facts that had led to their parting.

The mirror image constitutes a serious obstacle for mediators. One of their major tasks is to smash or at least crack it; but it is constructed of emotional plate glass.

Chapter Five
Acceptance

The first and in some senses continuing difficulty for mediators is acceptance. To do their job with any effect they must be believed to have various qualities. First, of course, they must be trustworthy; it must be recognised that nothing told them will be passed on to anyone without permission. They must be impartial; whatever their private feelings, they must never abuse their position of trust by doing or saying anything to suggest preference of one side over the other (the marriage counsellor is in much the same position). They must be well-informed and judicious; any comments they make must be apt and realistic. They must be friendly and feel genuine good will towards both parties even if occasionally distressed by their actions.

Acceptance comes about in various ways, sometimes gradually, sometimes, as I shall shortly recount, quite rapidly. But, as I have often been asked, how does it start?

The intervention of mediators may be requested by one or possibly both parties. But even so, unless the mediators are somewhat improbably already well known to all protagonists, they are still on probation and must, as individuals, earn acceptance in the current situation.

More often in my experience, however, the initiative is taken by the would be mediators themselves. Someone becomes deeply concerned about a particular situation and discusses the possibility of mediation with friends and colleagues. If his or her enthusiasm is not then dampened, there will probably be further consultation with well-informed people including the British (or other relevant) government as well as local representatives of the hostile parties.

Potential mediators meanwhile are continuing to debate the issue with their own organisation. As some sort of initiative becomes increasingly probable, the practicalities receive increasing attention — funds, persons available for the job, timing, approach, and so on.

(I should say that I am loosely defining these stages as a result of my experience with both British and American Quakers, with whom I have been through this sort of procedure several times. I have no direct experience of how other groups set about making their decisions.)

The next step will probably be to ask the ambassador or other emissary of the states or groups (where guerrillas are involved) concerned, if a fact finding visit would be permissible. Except when the role of, say, the Quakers was already known and appreciated, it would hardly be appropriate to say anything about mediation. This would understandably be considered an intrusion — and in any case it is unlikely that a firm decision could be made before the visit. So reference to the fact finding mission is perfectly truthful and the proposal is usually likely to be approved. (This, however, might not be so if the group, or occasionally individual, were not known to be serious and responsible).

So the visit is paid. The travellers return home to report and a final decision is made to go, or not to go, ahead. Resources are allocated and a team assembled (or, rather, a usually flexible — for not everyone can always be spared to go — arrangement is made about who would be available to go and when).

However, by the time the reconnaissance group has returned and the ultimate green light flashed, it is possible that something will have happened to point the way forward fairly clearly.

On one such mission, my colleague and I were, until the day before we were due to leave, increasingly depressed by the situation. We had met the president of the country involved and a number of people who held high office or were well informed — occasionally both. From these we gained the impression that the authorities were extremely unlikely to alter what appeared to us to be disastrous policies. I had in fact already drafted a report saying that the effort to mediate would be fruitless because at least one of the contestants had no desire for a settlement that would inevitably involve compromise.

Then, however, we met the powerful minister most directly concerned with the situation and the conduct of the hostilities. When my friend and I started to explain that we were Quakers and......, he interrupted. 'I know all about Quakers' he said. 'I've been to a couple of their seminars. Why don't you try to organise some meetings to bring the two sides together?'

So a PS was added to the report and a long period of mediation was begun.

This, however, was a somewhat unusual course of events. Although I don't have a statistically valid sample of cases, it seems more usual that mediation begins without any official request or suggestion on either side. The start of our work in relation to the Nigerian civil war of 1967-1970 illustrates both this fact and several other points of possibly general significance. Some readers may remember this as the Biafran war, a particularly horrific conflict in which perhaps as many as a million people, mainly the young and the old, died of starvation. It was fought between the break-away Eastern Region, in which the predominant tribe were the Ibos, who strove to gain independence as the state of Biafra from the rest of Nigeria and, after atrocious suffering, failed.

I was personally implicated because I had lived and worked for three years in West Africa a few years previously, and still had some responsibility for an experimental school in the Western Region. (These Regions were subsequently broken up into many more and much smaller States, and the old topographical names have only historical significance).

In the late winter of 1966 a series of ominous signs, bloody coups, massacres, the hardening of attitudes on both sides, the angry clamour of the media, made it clear that conflict was imminent. At this stage, John Volkmar and I went on a reconnaissance to Nigeria; we returned full of foreboding. One particular incident made me certain of the worst.

One day we visited a wise and noble old Ibo gentleman, Sir Francis Ibiam. He was a physician, a former governor of the Eastern Region who had also been a high officer of the World Council of Churches (and not long after he renounced his English title and first name, replacing the latter with Akanu). By this time, Enugu, the capital, and the rest of the Region were as cut off from the rest of Nigeria as was possible without the actual declaration of war. To get there endless road blocks had to be passed, an uncomfortable process as the soldiers manning them were high on palm wine and armed with automatic weapons which they waveringly held to our stomachs while asking hostile questions. So things were pretty far gone and, looking back, it was easy to see how the present pass had been reached through a fateful sequence of provocations followed by counter-provocations, each one digging the grave deeper.While we were with Ibrim, he received a message to say that a group of young Ibos had hijacked a Nigerian Airways plane at Benin airport and flown it to Enugu. It seemed to us obvious that this 'peace time' act of piracy was likely to be if not the very last, at least one of the last few straws. Surely, I thought, someone so wise and humane as Ibiam, though a loyal Ibo, would recognise with dread the probable consequences of this event.

Not a bit of it. He bounced from his seat and, unable to contain his glee, danced round the room chortling at the impudent courage of the young Ibos.

We left heavy hearted and reported back to Philadelphia. We did so on the day that the Six Day War erupted in the Middle East. A grim session.

We did nothing much for the next few months. We kept in general touch with the situation, but there did not appear to be much chance of doing anything more positive. Then John, who worked in Africa, visited Niger and happened to meet President Hamani Diori, who was a member of the consultative committee on the war chaired by Emperor Haile Selassie, which had been set up by the Organisation of African Unity (OAU)). Diori was extremely frustrated that they could do absolutely nothing because, since Nigeria was a member state of OAU and the war an 'internal' matter, they had no access to what was then temporarily Biafra. But, he said, the Quakers suffered no such restraints and should now consider getting into the act once more. What he suggested specifically was that the Quakers might try to arrange a secret meeting of officials to search for possible common grounds of agreement. Confidentiality was essential as one or two other initiatives had been spoiled by premature publicity.

(I might emphasise here that since most of today's approximately 30 wars are civil wars about which the UN and regional bodies such as the OAU are unable, at least officially, to take any action, there is considerable need for the non-official agencies to fill the gap. This is doubly desirable since many of these wars, though intranational, often have serious international implications).

So we held a further series of meetings with the relevant people. I made a trip to Geneva for discussion with the Quaker representative at the UN to discuss a possible venue for the suggested meeting and the problems of maintaining both security and secrecy. I was encouraged to hear that the Austrian Chancellor Kreisky had offered us the use of an Austrian state castle and it is one of my minor regrets that as the meeting never took place, I never stayed in the castle.

Having completed these preliminaries, we went to Lagos to discuss Diori's idea with the Nigerian authorities. John was supposed to be coming, but he was ill and I was accompanied instead by Walter Martin, then with the Quaker UN Office in New York, later the General Secretary of the Friends Service Council in London and subsequently of Quaker Peace and Service.

It was clear that the proposal we were hoping to present was important and would have to be agreed at the highest level. But General Gowon, was inaccessible. Various well placed people, including the Secretary of the Cabinet, Hamzat Ahmadu, tried to arrange a meeting, but the message always came that it had been vetoed by a Mr King. We had no idea of the identity of Mr King, but imagined some shadowy hang-over from the colonial period, a sort of *eminence blanche* who was clinging on to his shreds of power.

Finally, however the matter was clinched by Edwin Ogbu, permanent secretary at the Ministry of Foreign Affairs who thought we had something worth saying, and arranged for us to see Gowon. (And then we also met Mr King, who was black, not white, a splendid man who became a great friend and had only been doing his duty by protecting his boss from the intrusion of busybodies).

The general was extremely pleasant and somewhat interested in our proposal. However, balanced and sensible though he seemed and I believe was, he was intensely suspicious of his enemies. He was particularly afraid that the rebels, as he called the Biafrans, might get the impression that he was losing his nerve and looking for some escape route from the conflict. In addition, he thought that our visit might be publicised in a way suggesting our support for their cause; this would harm our image as impartial persons concerned in general about the suffering caused by the hostilities to human beings on both sides. To this we could only say that we would be as careful as possible.

The general then went on to warn us that since we would have to fly on one of what he called the rebels' pirate planes, his forces would be trying to shoot it down. He regretted that he could not make any exceptions for us— in any case, he would not know on which plane we would be flying. We said we understood and were prepared to take the risk.

He then gave us a message to give to Colonel Ojukwu, the Biafran leader: in the event of a cease fire being agreed, he would bring in troops from a third party to monitor the lines. This was in fact a somewhat significant new idea. He also gave us personal messages for some of the Biafran army officers who were old friends, and told us that, if we returned safely, he would be very interested to hear what had transpired.He struck us as friendly, unpretentious and very able. We parted warmly.

It was in this way, with nothing specific spoken about it, that our work of mediation began. Our role as mediators soon became accepted and utilised by both protagonists, lasting until the end of the war nearly two years later.

So we made our visit. This entailed flying north from Lagos to London, hanging around until the Biafrans gave clearance, then flying down to Lisbon and several more days of hanging around for an available flight. Then, at 3.30 one morning we boarded a ramshackle old Superconstellation, full of war matériel except for a few passenger seats in front, and chugged around the coast of Africa all day except for a brief break at Guinea Bissau for a good straightforward meal of eggs and chips. (At that time Portugal was still a colonial power, and Guinea Bissau one of her colonies; no plane originating in Portugal was allowed to over-fly any independent African country.) As darkness began to fall we turned eastwards over the mangrove swamps of the Niger delta. Since there might have been night fighter planes on the prowl, our lights were turned off and radio silence was observed, although we could still receive messages. But we got lost in the mists. The pilot was afraid that the radio beacon we were following was a false one leading us over the anti-aircraft batteries. So we turned back and spent the night on the then Portugese island of Sao Tomé. Next evening we flew without trouble into Biafra, landing at the small airport at Port Harcourt. (Later, when Port Harcourt was captured, planes landed on the more precarious Uli airstrip. This was a widened roadway concealed by palm fronds in day time; the planes spiralled very steeply downwards towards it to avoid anti-aircraft fire, only switching on their lights at the last moment. In fact the Nigerian air force gained very accurate information about Uli and frequently bombed it. A friend of ours, an Irish Catholic priest, was badly wounded in one of these raids. He had previously been captured and tortured because when he said he was a missionary, it was thought he was admitting to being a mercenary and his captors were trying to extract military information that he did not possess.)

After some days in Biafra, the process was reversed: around the long coast line of Africa we flew, on up to London and then down to Lagos; a long route to travel the 300 or so miles between Biafra and Lagos.

Once in Lagos we were immediately given an appointment with the general, who introduced us to several of his commanders and senior officials. We were surprised at his cordiality and the frank manner in which he discussed the situation. He was interested, he said, in what we had to say, telling us that there had been no reference on the 'rebel' radio to our visit, which he thought demonstrated two things: firstly that we had shown our trustworthiness by avoiding self-advertisement and loose talk; secondly that the Biafrans wanted to use us as channels of communication and so refrained from making propaganda points out of our visit.

It seemed we had passed some sort of test, for this was the beginning of a very friendly relationship with Gowon which lasted until the end of the war. Although we never had the same closeness with Ojukwu, we were on equally close terms with a number of his ministers and top officials.

I have told this story to illustrate one way in which mediators may come to be accepted for their delicate and confidential role. The fact that we had been ready to face a certain amount of discomfort and even danger without making any personal profit had speeded up a process which often takes a longer period of demonstrating friendliness and reliability. During this probationary period, moreover, any lapse may prove fatal to the fragile relationship. Even when the relationship is very much stronger, however, the tensions of war make it to some extent vulnerable. Later in the conflict we had proof of this. The American Friends Service Committee, which sponsored our work, had a department concerned with emergency relief and was giving medical and other support to Biafra. But because of the extreme confidentiality necessary for the mediation, very few even of fellow Quakers knew anything about it. Consequently the fund raisers for Biafran relief never realised the possible political implications of advertisements showing pictures of starving babies and emotive captions that might be— and were — taken as criticisms of the federal government.

The Nigerians were furious and my colleague in New York was soundly berated by the Nigerian ambassador at the UN. Gowon referred to the affair sadly, in the terms of someone who has been let down by a trusted friend. We thought the Quakers were impartial, was the theme; can we really trust them now? But one of the senior Nigerians said 'When we are most deeply hurt, we just keep quiet. When we are openly angry it means that the pain will pass'. And, after many explanations and apologies, it did; fortunately the relationship was fundamentally sound. On another occasion I was guilty of an error of judgement that might have brought a hopeful mediation to an end. In writing to an important official at the end of one mission, I said I could see no possibility of a settlement unless a particular demand of the enemy were conceded. I ventured the opinion that the price that would be paid in yielding on this point would be infinitely less than what could be gained if doing so led to a cease fire. The minister wrote back angrily that if I and my colleagues really thought this way, there was little point in continuing the association.

I had, of course, overstepped the limits of propriety for a mediator, treading on dangerous grounds of internal politics and aspirations — if I had been asked my opinion, it would have been all right to state, tentatively, the view I had offered. To present it unsolicited was, however, quite improper and suggested that I might have been affected by enemy propaganda! I replied rapidly and contritely that I was very sorry, and that the idea was mine alone and so not to be taken too seriously. In fact I was forgiven and sent a Christmas card in absolution. But as it happened, many months later after many lives had been lost, the government made the concession I had suggested.

This incident high-lights the ambiguous position of mediators. By definition they are people who are friendly with two groups of people who hate (at least officially) and are trying to kill each other. However much accepted, the lurking question always remains: how can they, who claim to be our friends, have a similar relationship with the wicked regime we are fighting?

During this ever-precarious and difficult process of gaining acceptability and starting to mediate, we discover what may be the major obstacle — if the bitter fruit of the three poisons can be differentiated — to success. I do not just mean the achievement of a hoped for outcome, but the change of perception that might lead to a change of behaviour. This obstacle is the dualistic illusion concerning the good self and the bad other, the 'I' and the enemy of the 'I'. Unless this deceptive vision can be modified, no peace can be achieved.

Chapter Six
The Crucial Relationship.

Mediators have contacts with many sorts of people apart from officials, from whom they gain insight into and information about the situation. But the crucial relationship is with those who are in a position to make fateful decisions regarding the conflict. Unless there is some warmth in this relationship nothing positive is likely to emerge from it. If there is any dislike or lack of trust, however carefully concealed by well-chosen diplomatic words, the lack of affinity will reveal itself and deeply impair the potentiality of mediation: no one is going to take the inevitable risk of a move towards peace because of what someone s/he does not fully trust has said.

The idea that we can choose or change our feelings about someone may seem strange. After all: 'I do not like thee Dr Fell/ The reason why I cannot tell/ But only this I know full well/ I do not like thee Dr Fell', but such feeling has little known and perhaps quite unreasonable origins: the half remembered loves and hates of infancy, the guilty associations of our failure to know our own nature. The result derives from ourselves rather than from a rational assessment of the other.

Moreover, when we label him or her as cruel, violent or oppressive or even as good, sympathetic and kind, we are making a judgement of them as a self-existent being. Beings they certainly are, but ones which, like the rest of us, exist in total interdependence on innumerable others, including us. Their relative reality is as bodies having the regular complements of capacities (as the five skandhas — see Appendix 'Who Am I?'). Their ultimate reality is Mind, God, the Buddha Nature, the Inner Light, Al-Haqq or whatever we term the state in which we are all united.

But supposing X and Y have committed atrocities or done us personal harm; how then can we avoid feeling rage or horror? It may indeed be hard, but I have tried to order my own thoughts and feelings in this way:

(I must pause here to mention a problem in writing on these topics. At the same time as I am trying to expose the artificiality of 'I', I am using the same confusing and misleading pronoun as if legitimately. Thus the blind lead the blind and one delusion denounces another. But I trust the difficulties of expression will excuse and explain the inconsistency. However, since I began to write, I learned that the Vietnamese for I is 'your servant'. If we bear this in mind, while of necessity using the pronoun, our egotism will be diminished.)

I calm myself with meditation until I am able to re-experience the sense of unity with all beings (the quest for reality is a constant struggle to remember, or perhaps we should say to remember to remember). I come to recognise that X and Y are not good or bad or subject to any other dualistic definition: like the rest of us they are ultimately divine, but some of the things they do, the quirks of who knows what illusion, may be what Buddhists call 'unskillful means' (and others call wicked), that is, set-backs on the path to enlightenment.

I also wonder how my particular legion of 'I's would have responded to the harshness, indignities, neglect or spoiling which often seem to have impelled them to respond in kind. Would I not also have been a member of the Provisional IRA or the Tamil Tigers, or the forces that opposed them?

Viewed from another angle we see that our dualistic judgements are upset by discovering pleasant qualities in those whom we had considered evil. Himmler is said to have been a good family man who doted on his children; how could this contradiction be? But this is precisely the point: it is never possible to define and label on the strength of one facet of the 'I'. And our friends have sometimes hurt and our 'enemies' helped us.

This may seem arid intellectualisation, but only when our thoughts are straight will our feelings begin to change. I find it easier to feel genuinely warm towards people I meet anywhere when I remember that we are all joined in the divine ground of life.

The following little story I find both charming and relevant.

An old lay brother who served as door keeper at a monastery was so saintly that he saw members of the holy family in anyone he met.

When every evening the prior asked him who had come to the gate, he invariably answered 'Jesus, Mary and Joseph'. The prior would express his pleasure at this news and then ask what earthly form they had assumed. He then learned that there had been a visit from the plumber, the baker or a lady dispensing tracts.

To conclude, I must admit that it is always so much easier to say what should be done, than to do it. I have often struggled with myself to overcome fear or revulsion or a displeasing sense of moral superiority. On looking back, however, I realise that since my first mediation mission, which was in relation to the Indo-Pakistan war of 1965, I at least realise what I ought to do.

Chapter Seven
Listening

There is, today, an increasing interest in the techniques of mediation and lists of do's and don'ts have been drawn up and published. However, these seem to me to have little to do with the central issues. Advice on the necessity of impartiality, of avoiding judgemental language and words that might give offence (like calling Gowon's enemies 'Biafrans' rather than, as we did, 'the other side'), of not promoting our own particular solution to the conflict, is like telling a psychotherapist not to shriek at patients or express disgust at their revelations. The principal aspect of mediation that I would call a technique is listening.

I quickly learned the necessity for very attentive listening. I realised that what my friends and I were trying to say was often simply not heard, especially at the start of a meeting or if the situation were particularly tense. A question or comment would, it is true, be answered, but not in any meaningful way. It was as though our words were filtered through a compound of anger, fear, resentment and preconception that radically changed their meaning. It was to this new meaning that the people we were talking with responded, often angrily and usually irrelevantly. What we said was often perceived as having a threatening or insulting significance, or a perfectly straightforward question would be taken as criticism.

During the Nigerian war, for example, the federal government were extraordinarily sensitive to the harsh judgements of the world's press, and the most innocent query about some aspect of the war would be taken as hostile. We had simply not been heard, but if we had answered with irritation, it would have meant that we, too, had not listened properly. We realised that to overcome this difficulty of communication we must say very little, certainly not argue, re-explain, or contradict, but to be inwardly still and as receptive as possible. This would usually enable the storm of emotion, common in men under great stress, to blow itself out.

There would then be a period of quiet, often an apology, and a resumption of rational and constructive conversation.

Listening, however, does not come naturally to us. We are obsessed with the noise of our own thoughts and can hardly wait until the other person has stopped talking before making our own little speech — which we have been too busy composing to hear what the other person said. Recall almost any party or committee meeting.

To listen deeply means several things. First we must prevent our mind from wandering (telling phrase) and pay attention to what is being said. Then we must listen to the tone of voice: if you ask me how I am and I answer dolefully, shoulders sagging and mouth down-turned, that I am fine, you get the right answer; but not from my actual words. There may moreover be some more subtle emanation that you can pick up. Paradoxically the most informative listening is not concentrated solely on the person to whom attention is being given. The hearing is opened wide with that person at the centre, but with other sounds — such as passing traffic — not excluded. No filtering mechanism is used such as we have to employ when trying to converse in a noisy room, but which reduces general sensitivity.

Our civilisation is altogether too loud to encourage accurate hearing. Most Africans are much more generous with their attention than Europeans or Americans, but the best listeners I have met are Native Americans. In several tribes, listening is an art specially taught to children. When my Native American friends used to visit me, they would always fall silent, Quaker-like, and listen. How else, they said, could they become aware of and respond adequately to my condition — as they always did most effectively.

To listen attentively is to act autonomously. The listener has escaped the determinism of the automatic, computer-like part of our nature. To listen is, so to speak, to turn off or at least to turn down the power of the computer. Thus as in prayer, so in listening we try to reach a deeper part of our being.

Moreover, listening does not only lead to hearing and understanding, but also to speech. If we learn to listen, we will often find that the right words are given to us. These do not come as a result of careful thought, but spring from our more profound sources of knowledge.

The importance of listening, then, is not only that we 'hear' the other in a profound sense but communicate with him or her through our true nature. For this reason very strong and positive feelings are often aroused in both the listener and the one listened to. In this way peace makers may reach the part of the other person that is really able to make peace, outwardly as well as inwardly.

I recall one dramatic incident. I had to visit the headquarters of a guerrilla leader in circumstances that were potentially dangerous. I was apprehensive, realising that if I were unable to establish rapport with him, he would probably suspect me of being a spy or an informer and become very hostile. I knew I must prepare myself well and, when I arrived, listen attentively. At first he was cold and watchful. Suddenly he smiled, ordered refreshment and said 'People don't usually come to see me looking happy and relaxed'. We became friends and were able to explore ways of using humane rather than violent solutions to the problems that beset him.

Chapter Eight
The Approach To Violence

Probably most of the church groups involved in mediation are pacifist; certainly this is true of the Quakers. Their work for mediation is a direct response to perhaps their strongest testimony, that against war and violence. It also, of course, brings them into close contact with those who have chosen violence as the means of resolving their conflicts. It follows that Quakers and members of other peace-minded groups undertaking this work must be ready to talk with the military, both regular and guerrilla, indeed to befriend them. But how do these militants feel about dealing with people who disapprove of the use of force to gain what they consider legitimate ends, and how do the pacifists present their pacifism?

They let it be known, but not in an aggressive or contentious fashion, that they consider war a bad way of dealing with quarrels and conflicts of interest and, if questioned, will of course give the reasons why. They do not, however, (at least in my experience) take the leaders to task for their part in the violence, nor do they express any opinions on the rights or wrongs of the struggle; to do so would inevitably imply bias. This does not mean, naturally, that mediators do not often feel greater sympathy with one side or the other. I have personally found that when moving from one side to the other, I feel more warmly for the one I am visiting at the moment, whose pains and deprivations I am witnessing. This is not to deny that sometimes the cause of one is more just than that of their opponents. However, where there is great inequality in this respect, mediation is frequently impossible and mediators must seek some other form of peace making — this will be discussed later.

Although mediators may have some trouble with their own feelings about which party has the greater grievance, their concern is with the people who are suffering as a result of the war and who never had anything to do with the pressures and subsequent decisions that brought it to pass: the maimed soldiers, the widows and fatherless children, the people who have been starved, bombed out of their homes, turned into refugees. It is for the sake of all the people irrespective of class, nationality and religion that mediators work for a peace that is fair and sufficiently acceptable to all the main participants to prevent a recurrence of violence. In saying 'all' I include also leaders and those who may be considered responsible for starting the hostilities; their burden of power, guilt and anxiety is usually onerous and painful.

We do not usually, I think, try to convey these attitudes in any formal sense, but in the course of a number of discussions the right impression seems usually to be conveyed and our approach understood. Once or twice when we have become friends with someone in a rebel group, we have been asked what we think about them; we are pacifists, aren't we? Then what do we feel about people who are fighting for their rights? I have always answered that I would never presume to tell people what they should do unless I were fully sharing their suffering and their danger. I have then sometimes added that (probably unlike my colleagues) I have been associated with a liberation movement and been held by the police for my pains.

Chapter Nine
Speaking The Truth

Most of us feel it right to tell the truth, if only because this is an essential basis for building and maintaining relationships of trust. We feel especially that it is not right to remain silent in the face of cruel or tyrannical acts; to do so is tantamount to telling a lie. But the application of this principle can lead to difficulties. If an over-zealous mediator, hearing of some scandalous deed, were to storm into the president's office and accuse him of infamy, the mission would be finished immediately (and perhaps in some places in the past, so would the mediator's life!). The conflict between expediency and morality is not new, but this is a particularly painful example of it. I have often had to suppress criticism of a seemingly wanton act of violence in the interests of not damaging a relationship through which all such acts might be brought to an end. Must truth, then, be sacrificed in the cause of peace? But this, it seems to me, is a metaphysical absurdity: real peace is synonymous with truth.

The answer to the dilemma is through the quality of the relationship between mediators and the leaders they are dealing with. If it is unpeaceful or even neutral the mediators' outrage alone will be heard. It will be interpreted as a personal assault on the tender 'I' of the leader, instead of an anguished expression of pain. As such it will be angrily repudiated. But when the relationship is founded on real liking and the anguished words are spoken without rage they will really be heard and acted upon. A dear friend working in Northern Ireland and in close touch with some of the most violent members of paramilitary groups would never mince words in reprobating their murders. But they felt his love, and listened, and learned.

And there is another twist to this psychological problem. If leaders know that we are aware of something of which according to our social or religious principles we should disapprove, yet say nothing, they may suspect both our courage and our integrity. This would not help our reputation as mediators. There is no easy way out of these dilemmas except to continue steadfastly to maintain peaceful relations at every level.

The following incident illustrates the sort of situation I have been discussing.

On one visit to Biafra, my friend Walter and I were taken to a market place where 128 market women, mostly with babies on their backs, had been cut to pieces by the sort of bomb which explodes into slivers of metal a few feet above ground.

When we returned to Lagos and spoke to General Gowon, I was still shocked by this happening. I felt an impulse to exorcise my revulsion through angry accusations. However, I took myself in hand in the manner I have described, realising in addition that the commander-in-chief at the distant base cannot bear responsibility for things done at the front — especially if the perpetrator is a relatively unskilled pilot flying at 500 miles an hour at tree top level and only too keen to get rid of his bombs anywhere and head for home safely.

Nevertheless, when I went to see him, I told him exactly what had happened. He was shocked and said he was very sad; that although they called themselves Biafrans, they were still his people. He paused, then added: 'But perhaps in the end this dreadful event will have served some good purpose.'

I asked him how this could be and he answered: 'They will realise that rebellion doesn't pay and so lay down their arms'.

I answered: 'Excuse me for saying this, but it has had the exact opposite effect. They are all saying: If the Nigerians are killing women and babies, who cannot conceivably be military targets, then the things we have heard about genocide must be true: they mean to kill us all. So we might as well go on fighting as long as possible, there is no point in waiting to be massacred ignominiously. And anyway, there's always the hope of a miracle'.

He took the point, and nodded sombrely. We were still friends.

This incident not only illustrates one of the problems of speaking out, but also of conventional military attitudes. General Gowon was a humane and sensitive man, but he was a soldier steeped in the traditional wisdoms of his trade: in this case the principle that the way to get people to do what you want (such as to surrender) is to batter and terrify them into submission. Paradoxically many commanders believe that their own troops respond to bombing and shelling with increased stubbornness, but can seldom grasp the fact that their enemies will do the same.

There is a second, somewhat different, problem over telling the truth. Leaders on both sides (or three or four, in some of the more complex conflicts) are always avid for information about what is happening in the opposing camp. Although they are usually too intelligent to ask crude questions about directly military issues — they know it would only embarrass mediators, who could not answer without forfeiting their role — there are other things that interest them. Anything that bears on general morale, on the food supply, on the reaction to bombing, on the manner and appearance of the leaders, will help them to plan their strategy. There is hardly any type of information that could not convey directly or indirectly something of military interest that could not be interpreted (rightly or wrongly, both being equally dangerous) as a sign of imminent collapse, of increasing will to resist, of the efficiency or ineffectiveness of bombing policy, etc. And clearly all such information might be used in planning future military action. This is something mediators would not want to have any hand in.

What, then, can mediators tell the protagonists about each other? For one thing they can, as in the example just given, explain the real response to such matters as indiscriminate bombing. And I would add that in this instance the understanding that fear rather than aggression made the Biafran resistance so desperate helped to create a climate more favourable to peace. In general mediators explain and interpret statements that are misunderstood. This may be because they have been reported out of context, or because each side projects its paranoia onto anything said by the enemy, or because they were intended for domestic consumption and the mediators had in fact been given a somewhat different version to convey. But of course there is always a need for caution. Mediators must make sure that their interpretation is as accurate as possible and they will often have to spend much time in discussion with each other and attempting to confirm their opinions in a variety of ways, before passing on what seems important.

Important in this context means likely to promote a just peace, not the victory of one side or another. The ultimate task of mediators is to remove those barriers of incomprehension, prejudice, ignorance, suspicion and fear that impede it. For the fulfillment of this task it is essential that the truth be known. I don't mean the truth about the military situation or related issues which might give one side an advantage over the other, but truth which is the opposite of illusion, a perception that is clear of confusion and preconception; this is a vital element in establishing the atmosphere for purposeful negotiation.

The later section on active mediation gives a number of examples of what this pursuit of truth means in practice.

Chapter Ten
Message Carrying

Mediators are perhaps best known as people who carry messages between embattled parties. The messenger is not a passive postman, but an emissary; not a plenipotentiary, but at least one who presents the other side's terms and proposals in his own words.

The message is not generally, and should not be, a written one. There is more than one reason for this, both for the mediator and the sender of the message. The sender should realise that a written message, unless its deliverer is impeccably briefed in presenting it, can be easily misinterpreted and do more harm than good. Also, something committed to paper acquires a sort of immortality; thus something intended as a probe to evoke a reaction may acquire an undesirably high status. On the side of the mediator, a written message, especially if s/he has not read or discussed the contents, can prove a grave embarrassment. In ancient days the bearers of bad news or unpleasant proposals were often put to death; they still tend to be unpopular and to some extent held to blame.

The psychological position of mediators is hard enough in any case, without being lumbered with this additional strain. I recall that once during the Zimbabwe conflict we were asked to take a letter, not knowing its contents, from someone in what was then still Salisbury to an eminent person in another country. We reluctantly agreed, and then wished we had not done so; fortunately, however, we were not given the letter. On any future occasion, I would refuse as a matter of principle.

The following example illustrates the task of message carrying:

One of the major conferences intended to resolve the Biafran crisis was sponsored by the Organisation of African States in Addis Ababa under the formidable and remote chairmanship of the late Emperor Haile Selassie. (I had met him once in Ghana, a nobly dignified figure as he stepped from his plane in built-up boots and ostrich-feathered hat; but in a lounge suit he resembled a lizard with a squeaky voice — 'Bonjour, Monsieur' he fluted as we were introduced.)

Three of us were waiting in the wings and, as usual, keeping in touch with both Nigerian and Biafran delegations. Soon it became clear that things were not going at all well; both sides made angry statements of apparently adamantine positions; there was no debate, no give on either part. Everyone was tense and preoccupied; it was difficult to have a reasonable discussion with anyone. The Biafrans were grimly obdurate, pinning their hopes on massive military support from France, although they had lost all but three of their major centres of population. The Nigerians, led by the implacable Chief Enahoro, were buoyed up by military successes and convinced that the Biafrans could not long continue organised resistance (in fact they did, for nearly 18 months). There appeared no hope of compromise and we could see nothing but an indefinite continuation of Biafra's anguish.

Then one evening we had a long talk with Eni Njoku, the chief Biafran delegate. We knew him well, having met him in different parts of Africa, in America and, in happier days, when he was vice chancellor of the University of Nigeria at Nsukka. He was in a state of muted despair, saying that he had proposals that could break the deadlock. He could not, however, make them openly because they would be wrongly taken to imply an abandonment of their position and a loss of nerve. Their only effect, therefore, would be to intensify Nigerian military pressure; the federal government would think they had got the Biafrans on the run, and hope they could achieve an all-out victory without any need to compromise.

Whether or not Njoku was right about the possible reaction to his proposals, these seemed to us to be reasonable and constructive. They suggested that Biafra (which would even be prepared to relinquish the controversial and inflammatory name) should be accepted as part of a Nigerian Union. All they asked for in addition were two measures designed to ensure the safety of the people, the great fear being a repetition of the horrible massacres that had preceded the war. These were, firstly, that they should be allowed some sort of military force (perhaps a 'home guard' or armed police) secondly that they should have some measure of international standing to ensure that any aggression against them would attract international attention and could not blandly be dismissed as a purely 'internal affair' (perhaps a seat on the board of one of the UN special agencies or one of the regional organisations) but since he could not present these proposals without eliciting precisely the opposite effects to those he wished, he asked us to do this instead.

There was no way in which we could present the proposals at the conference, at which we had no official standing, so we decided to return to Lagos. This involved flying up to Rome and then down to Nigeria. I remember the delight of a summer evening in Rome, where we strolled out for a good meal of pasta and a bottle of wine, sandwiched between the thin dank air of the Ethiopian highlands and the heavily steaming heat of Lagos.

Gowon was as friendly as ever when we presented and explained Njoku's case. He promised that the Biafran ideas would be given full consideration; then we left to return to America, where I was then based.

A little later we were told that there had been much discussion, but that the hawks had won. They said that nothing new was offered, it was all a trick, a device to gain time. So that, for the time being, was that.

But shortly after, one of us met the Nigerian ambassador at the UN, who had not heard what was going on. When he did, he was horrified that the Biafran proposals had been abandoned, maintaining that they did in fact constitute an important initiative. He flew at once to Lagos, made his point forcibly, and the debate was reopened. But by this time, the military fortunes of the Biafrans had to some extent revived; they no longer wanted the sort of settlement that would have satisfied them when things were going badly.

This also illustrates the vicissitudes of mediation. For the psychological reasons we have already discussed, because also of such fluctuations of hope and despair resulting from shifts on the battle field and the international scene, conflicts can drag on and on for years. Mediators must commit a considerable slice of their lives if they once start upon the work.

Chapter Eleven
Active Mediation 1

Active mediation is the term I have coined for what takes place *within* the relationship between mediator and decision maker. It constitutes the active efforts of mediators to remove obstacles to the next peace making step, negotiation. They don't do this, as I have said, by telling leaders what they ought to do; they are not qualified to do this either by role or by sufficient understanding of the needs of a nation or group. What they can do, however, is to try to remove or to put into perspective exaggerated fears and suspicions, to dispel rumours, to explain that what their enemies *say* is not necessarily what they *mean,* to argue that they are not the utter monsters they are imagined to be, in fact to change the perceptions of leaders to the point where they come to think that it may perhaps be worth entering into serious negotiations. Mediators are not passive postmen delivering messages; they are participants in the total situation whose task is to try to change it in a direction that, in general, *both sets of protagonists want.* I put it like this because, if there was not some desire for peace on both sides, they would not tolerate the involvement of mediators; they would simply be a nuisance who confused the scene.

(I should slightly modify this perhaps; mediators may sometimes be encouraged if it is thought that they can be used and manipulated to the advantage of one or other of the combatants. Indeed this may always to some extent be so, but it soon becomes obvious and if it seems to be a dominant motive, the mediators will simply threaten to withdraw. I have on occasion done so and the admittedly slight suggestion of manipulation has disappeared; we have no longer been probed for information of military significance or asked to convey veiled threats to the other side.)

To illustrate the character of active mediation, I have used transcripts of discussions at which I have been present between a mediator or mediators **(M),** and key decision makers who may have been presidents, prime or other ministers, or high civil or military officials **(P)**. I have so disguised circumstances of time, place and circumstance, fictionalising some and combining others as to make them unrecognisable — even to the participants. So I hope no one will waste time trying to identify persons or occasions.

In so far as I was personally involved in these discussions, I have been guided (though of course my awareness has often been much less acute than desirable) by the principles set out in the earlier sections. I have attempted to cleanse myself both of personal preoccupations of 'I', and of fear, aversion for or judgement of the woman or man I was talking to. I have tried to speak in a manner which was consistent with these attitudes and by so doing to encourage them in the other person. I was often aware, however, of the incongruity — by our perhaps distorted standards — of trying to convey a metaphysical or 'spiritual' approach in the context of discussing political and above all military matters. But this is perhaps unreasonable. It is partly because we have separated our public from our inner lives that both have suffered. Had we not done so, we would perhaps not now need to discuss war and its mediation.

P. I'm told you have been meeting Prime Minister W. How did he strike you?

M. I thought he was intelligent and realistic.

P. Well, I don't know him except through what he is reported as saying and above all what he does. If aggression and brutality are signs of intelligence and realism then he's just what you say. I only know that he hates me and my people.

M. I wouldn't pay too much attention to his public utterances. You know yourself the sorts of things a leader is expected to say in war-time — all glory and victory, blood and thunder. If I may say so, you have a good line in that sort of rhetoric yourself.

P. Ah, but that's different. He knows perfectly well that I'm a man of peace and want nothing except to live quietly with my family. What I say on the radio is just morale boosting.

M. Yes, of course. Nevertheless W. takes it as proof that you are the same sort of person as you think he is.

P. But that's absurd. Anyway his family means nothing to him.

M. That isn't so. He is devoted to his wife and children, but keeps them as much as possible away from the public eye.

P. That certainly doesn't help me to like him more. On the contrary, in fact. I can't understand how a man who claims to be fond of his family can commit such ghastly atrocities, bombings that wipe out hundreds of other loving families. It just doesn't add up.

M. does not quite know how to proceed. If he belabours the point that W. really thinks just as badly, and for the same reasons, of P. as P. does of him, P.'s ego might not be able to take the strain. There might be an explosion of fury which would blow his relationship with M. to smithereens. He decides not to say much at the moment, but to wait for some more propitious time to drive home the lesson of the mirror image syndrome in conflict situations. So he continues in a somewhat placatory manner:

M. War is such a travesty of ordinary existence. I am sure that when you, and no doubt W., came to power you had no idea of the exigencies your office would have in store for you or what the pressures of conflict would be like.

P. That's true — in my case at any rate. He, as the aggressor, no doubt knew pretty well what he was heading into and just went on regardless. He must carry the whole responsibility for what has happened since, both to my people and to his.

M. wonders whether it is worthwhile raising the philosophical question as to who to can be designated 'aggressor'. It is perhaps the case that W.'s people had fired the first shot, but what about all the previous provocations by P.'s? But then again, why had P.'s government (and its predecessors) been provoking; had they not been provoked? One could go leap-frogging back to the dawn of history without finding a final link in the chain of causation. We can never point the finger at a single guilty party; everything that happens is the product of the convergence of multiple forces of which some may only appear more directly responsible than others. However, the conventional illusions of war demand that rulers label their enemies as 'aggressors', and themselves as innocent victims of aggression. Once again M. does not feel it wise to make a frontal assault on P.'s sense of self: his 'I' has taken a battering from the failure of his last campaign and is in a fragile state. On the other hand, if P. wants a settlement, as it seems does W., the way towards it will be blocked if each leader sees the other as implacably hostile and negative. Perhaps, then, something can be said to weaken P.'s perception of W. as irredeemably evil and violent:

M. It's worth remembering the strength of the pressures he has been under. Both domestic and international forces have been driving him in a direction I don't think he really wanted to take.
P. Then he's a weakling.
M. I wouldn't say that. I don't think anyone in public office is entirely responsible for her or his actions. A leader's decisions, as you surely know much better than me, are the final outcome after much discussion and a good deal of compromise. He or she would quite probably have preferred something else, but it seemed more important to avoid antagonising the opposition, or the superpower concerned, or the aid consortium, or the generals, or whatever. But however much this leader straddles different interests, and maybe comes out looking wishy washy or indecisive, he's the one who has to be dealt with.
P. What are you getting at?
M. I'm saying one has to be open-minded about people and at least give them a chance to demonstrate whether or not they will be reasonable to deal with. If you assume that they won't be, you'll just go on fighting until you batter each other to pieces and lose all the things you were fighting for even if you end up by what's called winning.

This sort of discussion goes on, in different guises, interminably. M. has to go on struggling unceasingly with the profound suspicion, laced with fear and hatred, that both leaders have for each other. It cannot be dissolved by logic or by even the most irrefutable evidence that such feelings are ill-grounded. Only by constant reiteration of the arguments and erosion of prejudices in different contexts, and by pointing to specific incidents that convey a different impression, can a slow, and perhaps only slight, change be wrought.

***

P. You have talked about my having dealings with my enemies — even of having some sort of relationship with our enemies — the very last thing I want, to be truthful. The only relationship I'll accept is that of master to servant; I want to bash them into obedience. That's all.

M. I know you feel very bitter about what has happened. But when I talk about relationships, I'm not suggesting something I think you ought to establish, but something which already exists, like it or not. You are both locked into a relationship, a very bad one admittedly, because you have a common problem which you are trying to solve by fighting each other. War is just as much a relationship as what you had when you were arguing about it at the UN and had a political relationship and were exchanging ambassadors with them.

P. So what; where does this get us?

M. I'm sorry if I'm irritating you. I'm only trying to say that this whole disastrous situation only exists because of a common problem that relates you to each other— the problem of the disputed territory. I don't see how you can resolve it except through this relationship.

P. I agree with that at least; we will resolve it by beating those bastards.

M. I meant through co-operation.

P. Are you crazy; me co-operate with that shit? I'll beat his rotten army to pulp and then hang him. That'll solve the problem.

M. If you say so. But I understood when we last spoke that you were interested in mediation because you felt that to go for a purely military solution was too costly. Also it wouldn't be a good solution because you would be left with a sullen and rebellious population which would continue the struggle by sabotage and industrial unrest and perhaps later by a renewal of violence. I was proposing going for the sort of resolution that is more likely to stick and if you want that, you'll have to do it together with W. But if you really intend to settle the business by crushing them militarily — and don't forget they might win, you don't need a mediator. Just let me know and I'll leave.

P. Oh, all right; no need to be so sensitive. Now supposing I agree, what would be the next step?

M. I expect to see him next month. Is there anything I could tell him on your behalf?

P. (laughs) Yes. Tell him to jump in the bloody lake. I'm told he can't swim and would sink like a stone. That would solve everything.

M. Well, then you'd have to deal with Z. who would probably be much more difficult. He has always been hostile to the idea of mediation.

P. Seriously, I'm not sure what I would want to convey to him. I have let it be known often enough that I am willing to talk, but his only response has been to repeat his preposterous demands.

M. But did you make your offer in a way that he could accept?

P. What do you mean?

M. I mean did you virtually say 'talk or else' or tell him what you were going to demand and how he was supposed to reply. If so, then your offer probably seemed more like a threat; something which could never be accepted without loss of face.

P. Yes, I suppose my proposals might have seemed a little uncompromising, but what else can one do? If you show weakness you are done for at home and your enemies take advantage of you.

M. It seems to me that the sort of formal announcements of willingness to talk such as you have mentioned often don't properly represent a government's position; they are made for another reason than just negotiation, the propaganda effect on domestic morale, the encouragement of allies and so on. But surely there's always scope for flexibility behind the rhetoric?

P. Quite right. I could bend a little on a couple of matters. But how can I admit this without giving the impression of climbing down?

M. You don't have to make these points officially. We could deliver a spoken message that couldn't be used against you because, if necessary, you could repudiate it. For example, we could suggest on our own account that you were prepared to relax your stand on some issues. We might add that you would only do this if they, for their part, were prepared to reciprocate, a sort of tit-for-tat arrangement.

P. Do you have any ideas about where I might be prepared to bend?

M. No. We can't suggest what is best for your country; we can only talk about how to remove the obstacles to achieving whatever you think right for you.

★★★

M. I've just been over to the other side, where I had a long talk with the head of the military government, General Y.

P. What did he have to say?

M. He said he hoped it would be possible to find a way of bringing the war to an end.

P. What a hypocrite that man is! If he really hopes that, why is he stepping up his attacks on civilian targets and launching a new offensive in the north?

M. He doesn't really strike me as a hypocrite. I really felt he was a decent and honest man.

P. (grunts sceptically)

M. What he says about that is that he can't negotiate from a position of military inferiority and has to keep up the pressure on you.

P. (as if addressing a rally) I will never yield to pressure. We shall continue the battle until victory is finally achieved.

M. Yes, I'm sure. But I'm given to understand that both you and he would prefer a settlement to a fight to the finish. Such a course could only do untold damage to both your countries and unspeakable suffering to your peoples.

P. Well, yes. But what can I do if he pursues this course of brutal aggression except hit him harder to make him think again?

M. Unfortunately he then thinks he has to hit *you* harder still to make you think again. So we get a vicious spiral of escalation.

P. You seem to be suggesting that I am responsible for the increase of violence. I rather resent that. I've told you often enough that I'm seeking every possible way towards a just settlement.

M. Please don't misunderstand me; I know you are. But I also think General Y. is also. The trouble is that war is a trap. Once it closes, it's very hard to get out. As I see it, both you and Y. are caught. What is sad is that when people are trapped, their efforts to extricate themselves, like escalating the level of violence so as to negotiate from strength, only trap them more firmly.

P. I suppose there's something in that.

M. And there's a psychological escalation as well. The longer the process continues, the greater the reciprocal hatred and suspicion; the more both sides reject any peace feelers as tricks.

P. All right, but it doesn't help much just to be told I'm in a trap; if it's true, how the hell do I get out of it?

M. I should mention that General Y. several times said that he didn't think you were sincere when you spoke of wanting peace, just as you don't think he's sincere when he talks of peace at the same time as he goes on bombing your towns. So the first thing to do is something that will demonstrate your sincerity.

P. Such as?

M. Probably the most convincing thing would be something you don't want to do and, for that reason, have refused to do in the past. This would show that you are sufficiently sincere in your peaceful protestations to do something that in some way puts you at a disadvantage.

P. Well, his response to such an action would be that I was either crazy or scared stiff and pleading for peace at any price. And so would mine be if he committed an equal absurdity.

Once again M. is faced with the conventional, and destructive, military wisdom. Take a risk, however slight, for the sake of a peaceful settlement, and you are accused of cowardice or stupidity. Far safer, according to this doctrine, is to condemn thousands of men to the far higher probability of slaughter and mutilation through a mindless continuation of the war. In any case, as M. goes on to argue, the slight military disadvantage possibly derived from, say, a cease-fire, can be effectively guarded against. M. continues:

M. The consequences you fear could be largely avoided. It would all depend on what was done, how it was done, and how the idea was presented to the other side.

P. Say a bit more about this.

M. Of course, it would be entirely up to you to choose whatever confidence-building step you chose to take — an exchange of wounded prisoners, opening up a corridor for relief trucks, inviting Amnesty or the Red Cross to inspect your POW camps, no bombing of civilian targets for a given period, something comparable .We would be happy to go and explain to Y.

P. Thanks, but I'm still pretty dubious. Y. might still think that any move towards peace is a sign of weakness. I've got him on the run, he would think; I must hit him harder and push him further.

M. I really don't think there's much danger of that. Anyhow, you can demonstrate both your sincerity and your strength by letting it be known that while offering a cease-fire or whatever, you were also preparing to take very tough measures if Y. didn't reciprocate, or tried to take advantage of you.

P. But I still don't see why I should take the first step.

M. In fact, you don't. I had a similar conversation with Y. who said more or less the same things as you. So he might come up with a proposal any day. But that sort of thing is hard to synchronise; in practice someone has to set the ball rolling.

P. I still think it would give an impression of weakness.

M. I really doubt it, especially if you took the precautions we have considered. But I look at it the opposite way. To take some risk for the sake of peace would seem to me a sign of strength, of the courage to take a chance.

P. So you admit there is a risk?

M. Oh, yes, of course; everything you do in war is risky — including doing nothing or making the automatic conventional response. But its really a question of odds. In this case you might lose a little if things went wrong. But if things went right, you might gain peace. So it could be a worthwhile gamble.

P. Perhaps.

★★★

M . I was talking to Colonel F. last week. It struck me that there was really very little separating his position from yours.

P. You amaze me. How could that be?

M. He says that now the only real issue between him and you is the strip. If you would agree to internationalise it, put it under a UN mandate perhaps, he would give up his claim to it and of course withdraw his troops.

P. (angrily) His claim? Ridiculous. Its our territory.

M. Well, as you know, of course, F. claims it too, and this would seem a suitable compromise. After all, it's only a few square kilometres of semi-desert inhabited seasonally by a handful of

nomads. Infinitely more people would die if both sides continued
struggling to occupy it.

P. It's a matter of national honour, something about which we will
never compromise. I'm sorry you have been influenced by their
propaganda. I had counted on you to see the justice of our case, or
at least to be impartial.

M. realises he has stepped out of the mediators role by making a
policy suggestion, especially one favouring a proposal from the
other side. If he had been asked, it might have been legitimate for
him to give his opinion that the saving of life would have been well
worth the loss of control over so small an area having no strategic or
economic importance. But even this might have been going too far:
in general mediators do not state preferences even if asked; if there
is a choice between courses of action, they will try to identify their
probable consequences, but in a neutral fashion leaving it open to
the combatants to make their own decision. So on this occasion
there is nothing for M. to do except apologise:

M. I'm sorry. But you know we only work out of concern for the
suffering caused by conflict and sometimes fail to take adequate
account of national policy and aspirations. But we are always glad
to be put right. And I can assure you I wasn't influenced by
anything Colonel F. told me; it was my own bad idea.

P. nods forgiveness, which is lucky, for M. had really spoken out
of turn. Nevertheless, he did have a valid point. Here was a
suggestion for compromise which, face, national pride, and ego
apart, was perfectly reasonable. It would save precious lives and
much misery, no valuable territory would be lost, while the few
nomads, if they cared at all under whose national sovereignty they
lived, would probably be better off. But his approach should have
been cautious, gradual and indirect. He should have tried to steer
the discussion so that P. began to talk about F.'s suggestion. M.
could have set the stage for a more reflective and objective
assessment of it by praising, and with some reason, P's realism,
humanity and care for his people; not because P. is particularly
susceptible to flattery but because, like many other leaders, he is

tense, needs reassurance and is apt, in this state, to react in an angry and extreme way. M. should then try to start a more relaxed and general conversation in which P. might say for himself what he rejected when told by another.

***

P. I find it most puzzling. You say that N. wants to edge towards negotiation, but if so, why doesn't he make some sort of answer to the terms I have suggested? I don't expect him to agree to all of them, at least not right away. But complete silence seems to me tantamount to rejection.

M. It could be interpreted that way, but President N. told us a few days ago that he couldn't find a satisfactory way to answer. Some of his advisers told me the same story independently — we don't believe they were all having us on.

P. But why? What's so difficult?

M. They said your proposals were so unresponsive to what they were demanding that there was nothing to be said. One of them put it like this. Suppose a man is sick with pneumonia and you give him a sulfur drug, which was considered a miracle before the time of penicillin, then you are at least responding, even though a bit inadequately, to his needs: if you show this way that you are fairly sympathetic, he may hope to persuade you to give him an antibiotic instead. But if you give him an aspirin, well, that has nothing whatsoever to do with pneumonia and shows you have no understanding of his illness whatsoever.

P. I can't believe my proposals were so irrelevant. I really can't understand what N. is up to. If he really doesn't like my offer, which I personally think is generous, why doesn't he say so and state his terms clearly. Then we could get down to business.

M. There are perhaps two things here. They say they have always made it quite clear what they are fighting for; they have done so in general terms of principle using such words as sovereignty and autonomy. However, they seem scared of trying to express the general in terms of the specific — frontier demarcations, relations within the regional economic organisation — things like that.

P. Why be scared of that?

M. They have told me, and asked me to convey to you, that they are not pressing for all the territory you have assumed they claim; for example, they would not expect autonomy for the northern islands. But they don't want to make this public until a settlement is in sight, otherwise their people might feel short-changed — but if a reasonable agreement were in the offing they would feel satisfied.

P. I think its all very muddled and confusing. I don't see what I can do.

M. What they would like you to do is to come up with a whole set of new proposals, something they could feel was more like the sulphur drug, or even the antibiotic.

P. They must realise that would be politically impossible, out of the question. And that's why I think N. keeps stalling on talks. I'm convinced, and my intelligence people have some evidence for this, that they are going to go for the military solution. And of course that means that I shall have to also.

M. We agree that its very confusing. If we were you, we would probably draw the same conclusions. But knowing President N. and a lot of his people we find it hard to disbelieve them. They say they are also confused. They say they can't understand why, if you want to negotiate, you don't make an offer that you can both then discuss and haggle over. That makes them think that *you* intend to go for a military solution.

P. But they haven't a shred of evidence for that.

M. Once the suspicion is there, little evidence is needed by them — or for that matter, if you will excuse me, by you. Any tough speech, any movement of troops, any arms purchase provides proof.

P. Then what's to be done?

M. We think N. is mistaken not to present more precise terms, but if we can assure him that you would be prepared to consider them seriously it's quite possible that he would. It would be helpful if you could send a message.

P. I'll think about it.

M. We don't necessarily mean a direct message, but a statement in a speech perhaps, preferably one of which we could give him advance notice, saying something less implacable than usual.

Possibly you might hint that you would welcome talks if he would respond to your overtures.

P. We'll discuss it at the next cabinet.

Chapter Twelve
Active Mediation 2

P. We were very disappointed at the collapse of the conference.

M. Why do you think it failed?

P. They just shouted slogans at us; refused to discuss our proposals. There was no real negotiation whatsoever. We did our best and are now feeling most discouraged. We can't see any way forward.

M. Perhaps it wasn't the right sort of meeting?

P. What else could we have done?

M. It may have had too much publicity. They were not only shouting these slogans at your delegation, but at their own people and the world's press. They may have felt, in fact they suggested this to us, that it wasn't an atmosphere where they could have been easy discussing complicated details; so all they could do was to state their case as clearly and unequivocally as they could.

P. And so waste an opportunity of ending the whole miserable business.

M. Well, as so often, we have to remember their internal affairs. As you know, they depend on the collaboration of the opposition party to hold things together and the opposition are, if anything, more extreme than the government. I'm convinced the government really want a settlement but are afraid that a long-drawn-out negotiation, in which there would necessarily be accommodation on both sides, could make things very hard for them at home.

P. So the whole thing was a farce!

M. Not exactly. They made their point as toughly as they could, which was useful domestically, and at the same time there was just a chance that something more positive might have come out of it.

P. I don't see how.

M. Nor do I, but people tend to hope for miracles.

P. Well, I'm certainly not going to set up any more conferences just to improve their local status.

M. What about waiting until the dust has settled somewhat and then trying to arrange a quite different sort of conference?

P. What sort?

M. An entirely secret and unpublicised one — no press, no communiqué, tight security.

P. Even if you're right it would be very hard to arrange. Everyone would be aware of a group of prominent figures converging on some locale.

M. I'm not saying it would be easy. However, I was going to suggest that a new cycle of discussions might begin with second-level people; senior officials rather than ministers, who might be less noticeable. And it might be better from another point of view; they might not be so pressured to make political points, and so be more able to get down to the hard tacks of detail.

P. Yes, that's right. Also, to be cynical, if they make a cock-up of things, the top leadership won't be so clearly implicated. Could you help?

M. Perhaps. We might be able to arrange a meeting of this smaller, less conspicuous type, but one at a higher level and on a larger scale would be beyond the resources of a non-official body such as ours.

P. But that might come later after a preliminary get-together had cleared away some of the obstacles.

M. That's right. You see, I think another flaw of the last meeting was that there wasn't enough preparation; both sides jumped into the main issues before they were ready and before there was the necessary minimum of mutual understanding.

★★★

P. I really don't understand you people. You maintain that you don't get any profit from all this travelling around which must often be very tiresome and difficult. Why do you do it?

M. (expressing views which are not necessarily held by all mediators, but which illustrate the motives of some of them) We feel strongly about the great suffering that is brought about by violence — the destruction of lives and homes and often cultures and ways of life, and the mental anguish of people like yourself, who carry such an awesome burden of responsibility.

P. Do you think it's always wrong to use violence? What else would you have done in our place?

M. Yes, we do feel that war is wrong. However, the world being as it is, it is impossible to blame people for resorting to it. In any case, we human beings are all in some ways collectively responsible for it — we maintain political and economic systems that conduce to war. What we would hope to do, however, is to help people find a way of disentangling themselves from conflict, of finding alternative ways of settling their differences.

P. Do you mean war is against the will of God, or something like that?

M. I don't personally put it like that; it would seem to suggest that people who seek peaceful solutions are somehow morally superior to those who don't. But I believe we all of us, in one manner or another, resort to violence, hurtful ways of thinking or behaving, because we have a wrong view of human nature.

P. How?

M. We feel that we are self-sufficient and independent entities, but we aren't. Everything we do and think is the product of forces — other people, history, our education, the ideas that influenced us and our parents — acting upon us. And likewise everything we do and think is a comparable force affecting other people and events. Like sub-atomic particles in a field of force, we are part of a system, elements that are constantly interacting with and being affected by and also affecting all the others. The results of this incessant interplay are inherently unpredictable; nothing is sure save uncertainty, although of course, given a range of possibilities some probabilities can be reasonably identified.

P. I understand this in a way. But what I fail to understand is what it has to do with war and violence.

M. This. If we think of human beings, ourselves, as being separate entities, we essentially feel that we can order our affairs without reference to others; hence the obsession with our own interests, with what is right for *me*. We expand the principle to the groups we belong to or through which we operate, the family, the state, whatever. Although the superficial causes of wars vary enormously, the underlying ones derive from this principle. One group or nation attacks another one because it feels that its interests will be served thereby, or that if it does not, they will be harmed; or for the same reason it behaves in such a way, oppressively for example, that causes others to attack it. What both sides fail to realise is that hardly ever, except perhaps sometimes briefly, do they really get from war what they had hoped to gain.

P. If I really thought that, I'd have to resign, wouldn't I?

M. What I believe we all have to do, whoever we may be, is to realise that we are not isolated self-existent beings. We do something, which may be something on a vast and portentous scale, like declaring war, or a small and insignificant one, like leaving an unrewarding job, believing that these are isolated actions which will change one aspect of life by removing a nagging problem without which everything would be fine. But nothing will ever be the same in any area of our existence. The war will bring fresh problems in its wake; the unrewarding job will be succeeded by the miseries of unemployment....

P. You are a proper pessimist. What is the point of doing anything?

M. It's this. As well as the aggressive ego-drive that sets us against each other we all have a deep, if half-hidden, realisation of the truth that we are one, and an equally powerful drive to *realise*, I mean to make real, this unity. Hence the love and friendship and compassion which makes human society human. Once we recognise how our fates are bound *together*, we can look for ways of solving our problems together. But if we think of ourselves as lonely entities struggling against a malevolent force, things get more and more out of control, and go from bad to worse.

P. You mean that if we were to act as though we thought humanity was one and stopped concentrating on just one small fragment of it, the world would be a better place.

M. Yes. That's why I am against violent solutions.

P. But I can't see how that helps get out of our present troubles.

M. I don't either, in any specific way. But I will say this: most of your difficulties with General D. come from your profound distrust of each other. This leads you both to see insurmountable snags to every possible solution. You block every escape avenue with a barrier of suspicion. But if you could change your attitude towards him ....

P. Please don't ask me to love him.

M. I wouldn't dream of it. But, if I may say so, you do think of him unrealistically. I would just hope that you could both come to see each other with less distortion. You are bound to each other by one of the closest ties except love — you are trying to kill each other. Only by working together can you both escape this awful symbiosis. You may then find your common humanity stronger than your mutual hatred.

★★★

M. We visited the other side last week and they asked us to suggest that it might be a helpful move to have a temporary cease-fire in the southern sector.

P. Why?

M. It might cool feelings down to a point where negotiations were possible.

P. But the world knows, and they know, that we are ready to negotiate at any time.

M. I'm afraid they don't believe this.

P. Why not? Didn't I announce this at the General Assembly only three weeks ago?

M. Yes, indeed. But in the tense atmosphere of war, what people say counts for much less than what they do. They say that your expressed wish to negotiate a settlement was contradicted by your bombing of their second city the day after your speech.

P. That was intended to demonstrate that my quest for peace in no way reflected a weakening of my resolve. It also demonstrated the terrible consequences of continuing the struggle and not coming to the conference table.

M. Well, I am afraid it was misunderstood. The president simply said it proved that you couldn't be trusted, but reiterated a statement similar to yours — that he would respond to any genuine (he stressed this condition) proposal for negotiations.

P. No one believes a word he says, anyway.

M. Perhaps we should not be too hasty. Anyhow, after this, he asked to see us and then made the suggestion for the cease-fire.

P. I don't see the point of it.

M. I think it's this: the fact that you both dislike and distrust each other so much makes it necessary, if you are really interested in a negotiated peace instead of continued reciprocal slaughter, to make a gesture of good faith.

P. Very well, then. Let them cease their aggression in the southern sector and we will follow suit.

M. That would be as unacceptable to them as it would be to you. You would both be afraid the other would take advantage of you.

P. I suppose that's true. If there were to be a cease-fire it would have to be simultaneous and bilateral. Frankly, however, the idea doesn't appeal.

M. Why not?

P. How would I know that they would not use the opportunity to consolidate their position, and to bring forward more troops and supplies?

M. Perhaps that danger could be avoided.

P. How?

M. Supposing a third-party monitoring force were brought in; one set up by the UN, the Commonwealth, the OAU for example.

P. Oh, no. My cabinet wouldn't stand for any further internationalisation of the conflict.

M. I'm afraid that if you took that line then the other side would simply assume you intended to use the cease-fire to gain the advantage you fear that they would seek. In which case, if they hadn't already started, they would certainly reinforce their troops and strengthen their positions. The cease-fire would be a farce, unstable and temporary, and would merely set back serious moves towards peace.

P. So the whole idea can be discarded.

M. No, no. If you really want a negotiated settlement as soon as possible, the other side's proposal for a cease-fire is a good one. If it worked it would provide a respite during which bloodshed would be greatly reduced — and the fewer the killings the lower the unreasonable war fever — and preparations for negotiations could be started in an atmosphere of relative calm and purposefulness.

P. But suppose the whole thing is a trick? Suppose they are just making what seems like an reasonable offer hoping I'll either reject it, in which case they make a propaganda point, or accept it, in which case they use it to my disadvantage — which is what I suspect. I just don't trust them.

M. In our opinion the offer was made in good faith, and we believe that if it were turned down you might lose an opportunity that might not recur for some time. They would probably feel that a further period of fighting would be necessary before you were likely to accept another offer. But of course you would be quite right to take whatever steps you felt necessary to preserve the cease-fire intact.

P. You mean through some monitoring arrangement?

M. Yes.

P. It might be worth considering. How would it be worked?

M. I don't know much about that sort of thing, but I could put you in touch with people who do.

★★★

P. I'm getting really worried about the island.

M. Do you think President F. is really going to try to invade?

P. It looks like it. I have reinforced the local garrison, but the way F. is talking, that probably won't deter him. And that means war; who knows where it will stop?

M. There must be some alternative?

P. I don't think so. We obviously cannot yield on any issue affecting our territorial integrity; that's a matter of essential national principle.

M. I'm a bit cautious about that sort of statement. In their *Getting To Yes*, Fisher and Ury, who are friends of mine, say it's vital to keep position, roughly what you refer to as principle, separate from interest, and to lay much greater stress on interest.

P. I don't see how that applies in this case. My forebears annexed the island three centuries ago. It's obviously part of our interest to keep control of it and to keep our dominion intact.

M. Yes, I see that; but what price are you prepared to pay? Everyone is agreed that the island has no economic value. The people are linguistically and culturally closer to Exia than to you, and have been a constant headache to successive governments. One could in fact argue that it would be in the national interest to get rid of this worthless island and its unruly people; that the *principle* of hanging on to it is not in your *interest*.

P. That's absurd. If I were to tamely let go of the island, my government would fall and the Exians and every other potential aggressor in the region would think they could bully and blackmail us.

M. Yes. I see that. But what you are saying is that you are hanging on to a position or principle less because of the advantages it brings or interests it serves, than because of the disadvantage to your vital interests that might follow from discarding it.

P. (reluctantly) There may be something in that.

M. Please don't be offended if I take the argument a little farther. If, at this juncture, you stick to your principle of preserving territorial sovereignty with regard to the island and are forced into war, other of your interests will undoubtedly suffer. The economy will most likely be harmed, many of your young men will be maimed or killed — how many lives, one might ask, is it proper to sacrifice for a principle — and above all there is a chance that you might lose the war; one or other of you must. In that case everything would be lost — the island, the soldiers who fought in vain, no doubt your government would fall; nothing would survive but the principle that brought such disaster.

P. You are certainly frank. My grandfather would have had you shot! But the whole idea sickens me too. What can I do, though? We are trapped in a situation where I don't see how we can avoid war, that is if Exia goes on with this mad venture.

M. I'm not completely sure they do want to. I have an idea that President H. may feel as much trapped as you do. I suspect that the issue about the island has been artificially whipped up to distract attention from the worsening economic situation and that he is now horrified to realise that he has roused the tiger of militaristic chauvinism.

P. (sarcastically) My heart bleeds for the unfortunate fellow.

M. I hope to be able to discover more next week when I go to Exia. Anyway, if I'm right, he would welcome a let-out. A bit of quiet diplomacy might provide you both with an honourable solution to what is in fact a joint problem. I mean one which would bring you credit for wisdom and restraint,while avoiding the danger of abandoning principles without safeguarding interests.

P. What sort of solution are you talking about?

M. The details of course would be up to you. However, if you both decide to modify or withdraw from inflexible and irreconcilable positions — F.'s being that *he* must have the island, yours being that *you* must — and instead consider your common interests — avoiding the ravages of war — it shouldn't be too difficult to find one. For example, you might, on the generally accepted and respected principle —

P. Ha! I thought you despised principles.

M. (laughs) Not in every case — of self-determination, offer to hand over the island to UN trusteeship; or lease it to Exia for so many years, after which a referendum would decide whether it returned to your rule, or to the Exians, or became independent. Or something like that.

P. But the population is not much more than twelve thousand.

M. The same as some of the South Pacific nations. But the point I am making is that this sort of solution would have the advantage of avoiding confrontation without giving way to Exia, and at the same time making a generous and altruistic international gesture that would be widely appreciated. And for President F. it would have the advantage of changing the status of the island in a manner that would satisfy the most carping of the critics, and without war. I am certain the regional organisation would be delighted and do everything possible to help.

P. I still wonder how my people would respond to what the opposition would certainly depict as a betrayal.

M. Surely with relief. They don't really want war, do they?

P. (shakes his head).

To sum up, active mediation is the part of the process which is concerned with what might be called diplomacy rather than gaining acceptance, passing messages, befriending, and interpreting, explaining and correcting false information. These latter functions may well form a part of active mediation, but as adjuncts to rather than prime elements of diplomacy. This diplomacy is centred around the attempt to change the perception of protagonists concerning each others' motives, feelings and intentions. If they can be brought to see that these are less vindictive, implacable, irrational, bloodthirsty and aggressive than they had thought, they may decide to negotiate seriously, sensibly and constructively. This could lead to a satisfactory outcome to the conflict. If, on the other hand, they are brought together without this prior 'psychological' preparation, perhaps by pressure from a more powerful neighbour, it is unlikely that much good would come of it. This was recently illustrated by the collapse of talks, arranged by the Indian government, between the Sri Lanka government and the militant Tamil groups in Thimpu, Bhutan, in 1986.

Active mediation is also directed towards helping each protagonist to clarify and reassess his or her objectives. How valid are their war aims; what level of sacrifice is reasonable to achieve them? Such goals can easily obtain a sort of mythic sanctity completely unrelated to the true needs of a nation.

In general, mediation tries to break down the barriers that impede decision makers who basically hope for a settlement, from taking positive steps to reach one — a cease fire, de-escalation of the level of violence, negotiation. It tries to point out that some degree of flexibility, some capacity to compromise and bargain, is almost always essential. And it shows that such 'weakness' may be thought of as strength in the quest for peace. It also points out, that if one side compromises, so must the other.

Those practising active mediation must of course be hard headed. They must be aware that protagonists will vary in their commitment to seeking peace and that some may only make a show of so doing in order to gain a propaganda advantage. In such cases, and of course in those where one party is hostile to mediation, mediation is impossible (see Unmediable Violence, below). Finally, and very importantly, active mediation does not suggest the terms of any settlement. Its task is to remove the barriers to a settlement, but not to prescribe its actual nature; this is for the protagonists to work out between themselves. It is permissible to query the objections to aspects of a settlement as exaggerated or based on wrong information, but not to propose alternatives. To step out of role in this respect would seriously endanger the mediators' reputation for impartiality and hence their effectiveness.

Chapter Thirteen
The Effects Of Mediation

I am sometimes asked if mediation 'works'. This question opens a Pandora's box of issues. In one sense it is very easy to answer that, yes, it does in the sense that it has an effect. Any kind of intervention in a situation has results of one sort or another, but whether these are what one would have wished for or expected is quite a different matter.

The basic and most straightforward purpose of mediation is to create an atmosphere favourable to negotiation and so, in effect, to usher the protagonists to the conference table. But this is by no means the inevitable outcome; once the killing actually starts, irrational fears, suspicions and hatreds escalate to a point of near irreversibility. And on the rare occasions when a major conflict is halted in full blast by negotiation, no mediator can claim the credit, or even a significant share of the credit. Events have multiple causes; they are the product of countless strands of circumstance. If what the mediator is striving for actually happens, undoubtedly other forces will have been converging towards the same end. In only one mediation effort with which I have been associated, the Zimbabwe war, could the Quaker team claim any part in the final outcome — the major peace conference in London and the ultimately genuine establishment of Black majority rule (I say 'ultimately' because the preceding puppet government of Bishop Abel Muzorewa professed to have achieved this). I actually met a former American diplomat who had been attached to the UN during the war who told me, not knowing anything about my background, that it was widely recognised that the Quakers had played an important part in creating the conditions for a satisfactory settlement.

But then so had many others — other churches had shown intelligent and dedicated concern, other African nations, the frontline states and especially their chairman Julius Nyerere, the British government even though they strongly favoured Muzorewa as an easily manipulated ally, and many other groups and individuals, known and unknown.

(It is worth noting that the Lancaster House talks that ended the war and led to the establishment of an independent Zimbabwe were on a political and security scale that illustrates the limitations of the sort of mediation I have been discussing. Only a government could provide adequate resources. It is also noteworthy, however, that the Quaker group did continue its *mediation* while the *negotiations* were in progress because the same misunderstandings and false perceptions that had hampered agreement to talk were jeopardising their outcome.)

Mediation, of course, is not solely concerned with the issues of peace and war, but with all the subsidiary questions that sour relations, increase misunderstanding and give rise to suffering. Examples would be the famine caused by the blockade of Biafra, the serious economic and nutritional conditions occasioned by the ban on fishing in Sri Lanka during periods of the war, or restrictions placed on the work of the Red Cross which were seriously affecting health provisions. Apart from attempting to resolve some of these additional agonies of war, the great and constant effort of mediators is *education*.

This has many dimensions. The first is to create understanding in the minds of as many people as possible, the extras as well as the star actors. It is of utmost importance that they should grasp, intellectually and emotionally if possible, what is happening. For example, they should realise why their enemies are afraid of them and that much of their violence springs from fear rather than brutality. They should realise that their enemies are not monsters, but *human beings* like themselves who suffer equally at the slaughter of loved ones and the bombing of their cities. They should see how it is that the pressures of war make us all desperate and that in our desperation we are apt to become violent, vindictive, tunnel visioned and irrational.

A few years ago my young daughter spent the summer in Northern Ireland helping to run a holiday work-camp. One evening she met at a party a lad who had just 'found' religion and was expounding the importance of love. We should love everyone, he proclaimed but added, as though it was almost too obvious to be worth stating, 'except of course the fucking Catholics'. Mediators have to recognise and act in accordance with the essential human goodness of even the 'fucking Catholics' where and whoever they may be. This is not always easy; the ardent Zionist will not respond positively when I say that the nature of a PLO terrorist is essentially divine — or indeed, vice versa. I once gave a well-received talk which emphasised this point, at a religious gathering. A few days later, however, one of the audience said she had been thinking about it and realised that I had been telling her that there was 'that of God' (to use Quaker terminology) in a particular politician she disliked. When I said 'yes' she was furious.

But I am not suggesting that the job of mediators is to go around preaching. Nothing could be more irritating and off-putting, and not all of them share my beliefs. In any case, what we profess to believe is unimportant, it is how we *feel* and act towards others that matters. To the extent that we have loosened the hold of "I' and so feel deeper sympathy with the pains and confusions of others, whichever side they are on, we cannot help 'educating' them about reality.

Mediators deal with relative or conventional reality in that they aim to change outward circumstances. The vocabulary of their converse is that of military and political happenings. In terms of the ultimate reality these are all rooted in illusion, a faulty understanding of the world. But in times of great stress these are distorted by seepings from a deeper level of illusion. Consequently the logic and arrangements of 'normal' life are abandoned for exaggeration and fantasy. The 'reasonable' fears and worries engendered by war and violence change into paranoid myths fabricated from ancient hurts, pains and guilts dredged up from lower layers of consciousness.

Mediators are inevitably affected in the same way as the protagonists, less so, of course, though probably enough to understand why they feel as they do. They also understand that the combatants are almost completely ignorant of the way their opponents feel; it is a most important task, therefore, to help them towards this essential knowledge of the reality of the situation.

However, understanding of the reality of the situation and of the feelings of those involved cannot develop very far without self-knowledge. It is impossible to grasp that fears, for example, are illusory without also grasping that the 'I' which we believe feels fear is also an illusion.

How are all these different levels of education in the different dimensions of reality to be carried out? There is not very much to add to what I have already said about establishing befriending relationships with decision makers and others and about active mediation. It will have been noticed that in the latter there is not much talk about , for example, reality, or the 'I', or illusion. I have tried to indicate, however, that there is in general much friendliness, toleration, good will and concern, and embracing all these a set of convictions regarding human nature, its unity and its goodness. We can only trust that this approach is conducive to changes in perception that favour good sense and above all, mercy and compassion. If this, in great measure or small, is a more fundamental product of mediation than even a concrete result such as a peace conference, how is it to be assessed? But this, I fear, is almost less identifiable than any other result of the work. I can, however, tell one story based on what we heard, rather than anything I would have presumed to claim. It concerns, like many of my others, the Biafra war.

This war was conceived in a revolting series of massacres of Ibos, mostly in Northern Nigeria. After a gruesome gestation characterised by much bloodshed and turmoil, it was born in ill-disciplined fighting and abundant atrocities. The inhabitants of Ibo villages overrun by the federal troops were butchered and the Biafrans became increasingly convinced that a campaign of genocide was being waged against them. The conflict dragged on from July 1967 until early 1970. It was obvious that the federal army was going to overcome the Biafrans, but they were still fighting strongly until shortly before the end.

At this time I was in London on sabbatical leave with my family, and travelling to Africa from London. On about 7 January I had a telephone call from Arnold Smith, the Secretary General of the Commonwealth. As I have already mentioned, Smith was one of the many people with whom we had collaborated, exchanging opinions and information over the course of the war which, he now told me, was about to end; we hadn't expected it so soon, but the

Biafrans had made some tactical error and the federal troops had flooded in, bisecting the remaining Biafran territory. He asked me to go down to Nigeria as soon as possible. I was the only person he knew who was friendly with the leaders of both sides and I might be able to do something to moderate the massacres which, he feared — as did I — would conclude formal hostilities. Full of foreboding, I left as soon as I could.

My fears were groundless, however. As soon as I arrived at Lagos I heard that the war was over. As I said earlier, the fighting ended in friendship rather than carnage and the victorious soldiers helped the vanquished as if the vindictive savagery had never been. Within a remarkable short time those Biafrans who had had federal appointments before the hostilities were re-employed on full pay. If there was no vacant post for, say, a former ambassador, he was given paid leave until one became available. The atmosphere of reconciliation was almost miraculous; my Biafran friends were deeply moved. 'Why did we do it?' they asked in amazed anguish, 'What was it for? We lost a whole generation of our children for nothing. It was madness'.

We, too, were amazed and almost stunned with happiness that this nightmarish period — Biafra had been a hell of destruction, death and despair — was so wonderfully at an end. I was almost equally astonished when we were told by several people that we, and others following the same path, had made an important contribution to this outcome. But on pondering over this, I realised that we had spent a considerable amount of time in trying to educate the federal Nigerians and the Biafrans about each other, their fears and misapprehensions; about the fact that the Biafrans were resisting so desperately because they feared genocide if they gave in rather than because they were mad for blood; and that the federal Nigerians were not sadistic beasts using the hunger of children as a weapon, but decent human beings caught in the trap of war. If indeed our work had some effect of this sort, it was presumably channelled through a few powerful individuals who were in a position to influence many others.

But in the final resort, attempts to evaluate mediation are most unrewarding unless we are prepared to comfort ourselves with illusions of success. A mediation lasting a few years is as impossible to assess as a life. We must simply have faith that good lives have a better impact on the whole than bad ones, and that most mediators are able to do more good than harm.

Chapter Fourteen
Unmediable Violence

There are some types of violence for which mediation, as we have been discussing it, is impractical. For example, if the protagonists, both or either, are not serious about it there is no point in trying to act in the way I have described. There may be several reasons for their rejection of mediation. Their distrust of outside intervention may be excessive or they may just dislike the idea that others should in any sense be admitted to the intimacy of their affairs. Perhaps more often it is because they think they will get a better deal by going on fighting than by bargaining; indeed there is usually a faction that is of this mind even if the leaders favour negotiating a settlement — this makes the task of mediators difficult and even hazardous.

Factions certain of victory over their opponents are most likely to reject mediation. These opponents are usually oppressed minorities struggling for their rights (or, as in cases such as South Africa, majorities). The powerful oppressors certainly do not want any interference in their work of restoring 'law and order', and have little doubt that they will succeed. It is only when they are less successful than they had expected and feel the cold winds of fear and failure, that they will countenance mediation. So it was in Zimbabwe. When the liberation struggle began sporadically and on a very small scale, the white hegemony treated it as a temporary irritation. It was only when the fighting intensified with the formation of the Patriotic Front that they were forced to political manoeuvring — the device of a pseudo-majority government — and eventually to the conference table. This point has not yet, of course, been reached in neighbouring South Africa.

In 1971, when what is now Bangladesh was still East Pakistan, one wing of the whole country of Pakistan, I was faced with a dilemma. East Pakistan, nominally an equal partner in the nation with West Pakistan, was in fact a vassal province. It was controlled and economically bled — its jute earned most of Pakistan's foreign currency — by the West Pakistan-dominated central government. When the provincial assembly of East Pakistan voted itself a greater degree of autonomy (very reasonably, since it had the majority of the national population) the army, composed entirely of West Pakistanis, was sent in to crush any move for actual independence. There ensued a period of unprovoked carnage and destruction in which one million people are said to have died.

I was deeply saddened by these horrible happenings. I had met and courted my wife in East Pakistan and in addition was distressed by the behaviour of the West Pakistanis, among whom I had lived happily for several years. Consequently I was glad to be asked to go on a mission of mediation between the two halves of a country I wished so well. However, the more I thought about it, the more acutely my dilemma developed, and eventually, for the following reasons, I decided not to go.

I knew that the leadership in West Pakistan (which had much changed since I had been there five years before) was violent and obdurate. They were having no difficulty in imposing their will on East Pakistan, and I was sure that the drunken general (he had appeared on television while intoxicated — a shocking thing in a Muslim country) who was then president, would not have slightest time for mediators. If, improbably, he did have any use for us it would be as virtually his emissaries to urge the Bengalis of East Pakistan to abandon their futile resistance (a few bridges had been blown up and sentries strangled). If I had been able to meet the resistance leaders I could have tried to persuade them to give up this useless struggle that only brought terrible reprisals upon their people. If I had gained access to the general, I could only have urged him to moderate the intemperate ferocity of his army in order to avoid irreparable damage to the economic usefulness of East Pakistan. And in the most unlikely event that our efforts had brought the worst of the atrocities to an end, what next? The miserable status quo that had brought about the conflict in the first place would have continued; eventually, after a period of sullen passivity, there would have been a further outbreak of desperate violence and intensified repression. This, at any rate, was how I argued with myself.

Mediation may also be difficult if not out of the question in cases of great confusion, as when there is not a single struggle, but multiple conflicts. Northern Ireland is perhaps a good example. Between whom is a mediator to mediate: the Provisional IRA, the Official IRA, the British Government, the Ulster Defence Association, the Ulster Volunteer Force, various smaller and occasionally significant splinter paramilitary groups both Catholic and Protestant, the Irish Government, the various political parties? Unionist and Nationalist and others involved have at one time or in one way or another been in conflict with each other. Many would say that the core struggle is between the British Government and the IRA, but from this fundamentally unpeaceful relationship, which reflects the age-old unpeaceful relationship between the English and the Irish as a whole, stem many other quarrels that criss-cross the scene of life in Northern Ireland. Mediation as discussed hitherto in these pages, is impossible. Comparable comments might be made concerning the situation that developed in Sri Lanka after the advent of the Indian Peace Keeping Force (IPKF) in 1987. Instead of a relatively straight struggle between the Sri Lanka Government and five major guerilla groups (which, as so often happens with resistance movements, were squabbling lethally with each other) there were now three elements: the Sri Lanka Government, the Indian Government and the IPKF, and the Tamil Tigers, who had decided to continue the struggle. To these was then added a fourth, the revolutionary JVP, who were equally opposed to the other three — a viperous tangle of conflicts that defies any conventional approach.

What I did in relation to East Pakistan was precisely nothing. Now I think I was wrong. Fortunately for my conscience, the Indians resolved the conflict by invading East Pakistan, defeating the Pakistani army and thus opening the way to the independence of East Pakistan and the establishment of Bangladesh. But I ought not to have lost the opportunity to visit the area and renew my friendships with the many people on both sides whom I had known. One can never be sure, unless on the spot, how many opportunities there may be for service and for what I would call second-level mediation. I mean by this term, mediation which has no pretensions to paving the way to important negotiations, but which may smooth out relatively small scale pains and misunderstandings.

Such mediation may, however, actually lay the foundations for regular mediation once the political/military situation is more propitious. Our work in Zimbabwe was greatly facilitated because some of the Quaker team had known many of the Black African leaders and some of the Whites for a number of years. Thus, when the time for mediation was ripe, relationships of trust and friendship already existed.

In the case of Northern Ireland, where there is little chance of regular mediation between two, or even more, protagonists, there is always much to be done to soften hatreds, to explain fears and to ease hurts. Occasionally, if one is alert to the openings, it may be possible to contribute to some larger resolution. Such a chance was seized by Mairead Corrigan and Betty Williams, the women who won the Nobel Peace Prize for their determined and most courageous stand against violence. Other equally if not more effective work had to be done without publicity. A greatly respected friend of mine whom I will simply call K worked quietly as a go-between for eight years, in considerable danger and under great strain, until ill-health forced him to give up. I was privileged to be associated in a minor fashion with one of his activities which I can describe:

J believed that the fighters, primarily the provisional IRA and the UDA were much respected by the community, even if their tactics were not, for their courage and dedication to what they thought in their different ways to be in the interests of their country. He also believed that their joint concern for such non-sectarian matters as housing, jobs, public services and the future of their children would, if they could discuss them together, be seen to transcend what separated them. If they could then join forces on these issues, acting in some senses as an unofficial local government, they might together resolve the political problems; these, in the current situation of violence and rule by the British Government in Whitehall, could not be tackled properly. I was able to suggest at a high level to the British authorities that if the citizens of Northern Ireland were able to demosntrate a greater responsibility for running their own affairs and settling their own differences — now an impossibility, since they had no responsibility to exercise — the British could gradually reduce their measure of control.

I was much encouraged by attending a clandestine week-end meeting in which the 'hard boys' of both communities were brought together. At first they were wary and suspicious, but later, mellowed by Guinness and Bushmills Irish whiskey, had a friendly and constructive exchange. The British authorities also appeared to feel that this approach was promising. They were at this time secretly considering the possibility of withdrawing from Ireland, but were restrained by the fear of bloodshed that might follow. Consequently, any possibility that the two communities might together settle their own affairs satisfactorily was rather attractive, as indeed it was to the government of the Republic. But it all came to nothing. The responsible minister was promoted to a higher office and his successor had an entirely different approach which precluded all contact with paramilitary organisations. But I still think the whole exercise, or should I say series of exercises because J worked in this area of co-operation for years, was important and worthwhile. People met and came to respect and even like each other who would never otherwise have had the chance to. The value of these contacts and moments of sympathy can surely never be wasted.

So I conclude that mediation at one level or another can continue in almost all circumstances. Even if one is not shuttling between heads of state or other high officers, there are always other painfully unpeaceful relationships to be assuaged. This is intrinsically valuable and demands the same attitude and approach as international mediation to which, indeed, it may lead.

Resort to violence, though less so in the case of limited war to correct injustice or to thwart aggression, is a product of the illusion that such action can really resolve problems that arise essentially from ignorance of our own nature. This, of course, is true of all the ills that beset us. However, in times of violence it is hatred somewhat more than craving that is the dominant poison. As the conflict intensifies, so does the bitter unreasonableness of the hatred. I remember how, during the war in Sri Lanka, the feelings of the Sinhalese for Tamils grew increasingly exaggerated and grotesque. Such phenomena are sadly universal.

Chapter Fifteen
Conclusions

In the Introduction to this Part, I briefly mentioned a variety of circumstances in which mediation may be practised: in marriage guidance, in community conflict, between neighbours, between criminals and their victims, by high powered and very visible notables, by invisible nonentities like Quakers, both between and within nations, between workers and management, within institutions of every sort, by officials and by non-officials, over long or short periods. I certainly do not have experience of all of these, but like every other human being, I have practised mediation, had it practised on me, or watched it practised by others, in many types of situations other than those about which I have written here.

What all these circumstances have in common is the need, as the word implies, for persons in the middle, people who stand between those quarrelling with each other, trying to induce them to talk sensibly together. (Let me stress 'sensibly', there is no point in enemies meeting unless they intend to do serious business together and — eventually — to become friends). Such situations have, however, many things in common.

In the first place, the quarrel, disagreement, conflict of interest, injustice, oppression, or misunderstanding associated with the fractured relationship, represents a more fundamental disorder. The individuals or groups or leaders who claim to speak for the group, are acting out of the illusion of separation. They do not feel, or no longer feel, any identity with each other; they have no sense that by hurting each other they are hurting themselves. This exclusion of the other as the 'enemy' is something we take for granted in war, when we read with grim satisfaction of 'their' losses or the bombing of 'their' towns. But also in a marital break-up the sudden callousness towards a partner and the children involved is all to common. Formerly friendly neighbours become meanly unpleasant; work-mates, now on different sides in a union dispute, attack each other viciously.

The essence of situations calling for mediation is the spirit of violence. The dictionary definition of the word is the illegal, unjustified or excessive use of force. The violence may not be physical, but the violence of the heart, the ill-wishing of the other, can be equally damaging.

The emotional accompaniments of violence tend to make the task of mediators extremely difficult. The longer the quarrel lasts, the more its origins become swathed in hostile myths and fantasies. This is one reason why the conflict in Northern Ireland, which has lasted for hundreds of years, is so intractable, and why family feuds and vendettas in some parts of the world, such as the Northwest Frontier of Pakistan, continue for generations.

These fantasies are a source of fear, suspicion, resentment and hatred. All such negative emotions poison the minds of the protagonists, distorting their sense of reality. The work of mediators, whether faced with bitterly hostile married couples, or national leaders bound on mutual destruction, or workers and management engaged in a suicidal confrontation, is never easy; the shedding of blood marks a steep increase in unreason and in the obduracy of their task.

It may, of course, often be argued that it is not unreasonable to be engaged in a quarrel, whether it be domestic or international, physically non-violent, or lethally destructive; that aggression must be opposed, tyranny overthrown, the bonds of oppression broken. Few would deny that some causes are just and some unjust. I am simply saying, however, that when mediation is desired by the protagonists — which means that in some measure they also desire peace — the emotional concomitants of unpeacefulness greatly impede it.

I am also suggesting that whatever the circumstances, the mental obstacles to peace are similar in kind, though of course not necessarily in gravity. Mediators need the same psychological equipment of impartial good will, perseverance, imperturbability and objectivity; the same flexibility and preferably the same sense of humour whether they are dealing with a crisis in their home, or neighbourhood, or place of work, or are called in because someone's marriage is on the rocks, or because of an industrial dispute or an international war. The actual techniques and special knowledge that are needed will vary depending on the character and location of the quarrel. These, however, I believe to be less important than the attitudes and mental approach I have tried to describe.

The task of mediation, always, everywhere, is to find ways of reducing tension and enabling the opponents to stand back from the obsessive fears, suspicions and hatreds that have come to dominate their minds; to see each other and their dispute more rationally in terms of what is of real interest to them and others involved; and to consider, however sceptically, the possibility of mending the relationship and becoming friends who can together strive to make the world more peaceful.

This is when the process of mediation, as I have defined it, comes to an end. Now the protagonists must talk to each other (perhaps with the help of a third party), negotiate, and discover themselves how to solve their joint problem. Above all, they must learn how to solve the problems of *themselves*.

PART II
Social Change and Development

Chapter Sixteen
Introduction

We have been focusing on mediation, which is the most immediate — since it deals with wars that are actually going on — but not necessarily the most important, aspect of peace making. Omitting negotiation, the process of bargaining and compromising between protagonists, perhaps brought together through mediation, the crucial issue is the state of affairs that leads to war in the first place.

Many of the violence-producing circumstances are related to the conditions that normally prevail in what used to be called developing (which they weren't), emerging(which they weren't either), or underdeveloped (which they were economically by comparison with the wealthier nations), but which following my friend Walter Martin, I would prefer to call economically deprived countries (EDCs). Predominant among these are the residue of colonialism, the bad habits of the past which sadly were so often transmitted to the new incumbents of power after independence, the structures of authority and control favouring an elite and dealing harshly with dissident minorities (or sometimes majorities) who wanted something different; these structures were all too frequently incorporated into new constitutions kindly drawn up by departing imperialists and accepted gratefully by the local people in the faith that they would lead to peace and prosperity.

They led, instead, to internal unrest; to famine and favouritism, to capitalism and corruption; to a gap between rich and poor comparable to that between, on the larger scene, the poor nations and the wealthy ones. They led to war between those who were desperate to claim what they thought of as their rights, and those who were equally desperate to cling on to their advantages. They led to neo-colonialism, the economic stranglehold which the wealthy nations had over the EDCs, because the latter depended on doing the will of the former if they were to survive. Consider, for example, the fate of Ghana. This was one of the most prosperous of African nations on independence but she flouted the demands of the West (whose ambassadors are often little better than bully-boys) and became one of the poorest; coming to Ghana as we in 1959 did from one of the most chronically hungry areas of Asia, it was a joy to see such merry and well-nourished children, but not many years later Ghana's food supply was some 28% below the desired minimum per person. Domination by the rich nations, the North, led to the EDCs being laid waste as battle grounds for the proxy wars of the greater powers; consider Vietnam, Angola, the Horn of Africa, Afghanistan, Central America, the Middle East. These conditions were inseparable from hunger, instability and desperate deprivation upon which all tyranny can the more easily batten and so initiate a vicious circle of strife which further depresses hope and the possibility of peaceful and harmonious living.

It would, however, be quite wrong to think that problems of development, whatever we may mean by the word, as affecting only the EDCs of the Third World (a term Walter didn't like, but which I use because it is widely recognised). The economists and others who employ it cockily assume that there are nations that lack development and those, the nations of Europe, North America and a few others, which have achieved it (meaning that they are rich, powerful and of course usually unscrupulous). The state of the world convinces me, however, that these nations (I would except a few such as those of Scandinavia) are in no meaningful sense developed. They manipulate, dominate and greedily exploit the poor ones. They are full of a suspicious hatred for each other and so arm themselves madly, selling their surplus weapons to the EDCs and encouraging them to use these bombs and shells against each other. They neglect the poor and the unfortunate in their own lands, caring little that they are homeless, jobless and hopeless. If this is development, give me some of the peasant societies I have known before the wave of competitive materialism swamped them.

For some years I held a conventionally limited view of development. However, as I shall tell, the more I saw of the agonies of the Third World, and of the often responsible idiocies and moral aberrations of the First and Second, the more clear it seemed that if we were to talk of development it must be on a global basis. We must not simply be concerned with helping the poor nations — that could not in any case be done without changing our own ones. We must be concerned with a global transformation. There can be no development worthy of the name unless we dilute the venom of the three poisons in the blood stream of the inextricably interconnected world society.

Chapter Seventeen
Development

I imagine that my experience represents that of many others and trust, therefore, that readers will not object if I continue the early pages of this section somewhat autobiographically.

As a young man in the middle to late 1930s, before joining the army in World War II, I had wandered in remote areas of the Middle East and Europe. I liked the people I had met — the Lapp reindeer herders, the Egyptian fellahin, the nomadic Ababde, the Transylvanian peasants and others, but I thought of them as belonging to utterly alien forms of society that my anthropological friends called primitive. This word was intended not to denigrate but to describe a different and simple life style. However, it conveyed the impression of something steeped in tradition, primordial and unalterable. I did not feel that they needed, or would have liked, the comforts and amenities of 'civilisation'. Had I been asked, I would have agreed that they should have access to medical facilities and enjoy a reasonable diet and shelter, but not that their way of life should be radically changed; it was all right for them, the way of the 'noble savage', superior in some respects to ours (not that I wanted to share except briefly its picturesque and exotic squalor and lack of comfortable amenities).

This was the way the world was; some people were savage and primitive, some sophisticated and civilised. The latter looked after the former, preventing them from making nuisances of themselves, punishing them when they did and, on occasion, getting them out of some messy result of improvidence or ignorance; and doing heroic work to serve among them as administrators, medical officers, missionaries and teachers. There was, however, some doubt concerning the last two activities. My parents' generation explained to mine that Christian natives, especially if also educated, were often trouble makers, lacking the admirable loyalty of simple unlettered savages. There was no suggestion that we should encourage them to modernise — subsequently a popular word with developers — their societies and their economies.

But after we had picked ourselves up from the war, everything was different. Among other inventions such as jet engines, atom bombs and antibiotics, a whole battery of purposefully altruistic international agencies soon came into being. And with these last, the concept of development arrived. The countries of Europe (with a few exceptions most people were too polite to name), North America and Australasia (and before too long Japan, Israel and the border-line European nations) were recruited; and there were the underdeveloped countries, comprising almost all the rest of the world; a crude dichotomy indeed!

The developed countries saw it as their task to help the others to become developed, that is, more like themselves. Just how this mood grew I am not quite sure — I was too busy at that time putting my own life together. To what extent had a new sense of responsibility for less affluent neighbours been forged in the furnace of war? To what extent did we (or some of us) foresee the virtually complete collapse of empires (the first rumbles were soon audible) and the rich pickings for those who could wield the new technologies and improved communications in order to exploit vast natural resources?

I first came in touch with this whole range of endeavour during the late 1940s when I participated in a few short-term missions of various UN agencies; it was wrongly thought that my superficial background in anthropology was relevant. By the mid 1950s, however, I was deeply involved, firstly for three years an adviser on social planning in Pakistan and then as professor of education in the University of Ghana. By the time we moved to Harvard in 1961 I considered myself an expert in the field of the social aspect of development — a subject usually thought of in purely economic terms (as though having a sufficient income ensured a happy life!).

In 1961 I wrote a book based on this experience. It was entitled *Educational Strategies For Developing Societies* and was about the way in which education and other aspects of social development could contribute to economic growth. I wrote that I realised that there was an element of self-interest in much of the aid given by rich countries for developing the poorer ones — they would create new markets, they would gain concessions enabling them to obtain raw materials at absurdly low prices and sell back the manufactured products at disgracefully high ones. But I felt that on the whole this surge of new international activity was based on altruism, an increased awareness of need, a collective effort by humanity to share with and to help its less fortunate brothers and sisters.

This naive optimism flawed the book in many respects, though it became a modest best seller and went through several printings. Despite this failing, however, it was for its time progressive. It dealt with development not as a purely *economic* activity as was usual in those days: all other dimensions were considered only in the context of their economic contribution. I remember a Pakistani colleague who specialised in housing, complaining bitterly that a factory, a field or a cow were development projects to be planned for carefully, but that no one paid any attention to the human being who worked in the factory, tended the cow or ploughed the field.

I argued that, on the contrary, these material things were in themselves useless unless the men and women involved with them had sufficient health, were well fed, decently housed and, above all, adequately trained, educated and motivated. Following Galbraith and a few others, I maintained that development was about and for the development of *people*. To that extent, I was somewhat ahead of my time. Still, however, I thought of development in excessively economic terms. Those who thought as I did, believing that education and other social factors were major rather than peripheral elements in development, nevertheless referred to human beings as 'human resources' in the same way as coal mines, cattle or machines were material resources for development.

A few years later, when my book went into a new paperback edition, I was asked to write a new introduction. By this time I had no illusions as to the seamy side of international aid and development work in general, and tried to express this fresh understanding in it. But nobody seemed to recognise the contradictions with what I had written before, and the blurb merely said that I had demonstrated the 'continued relevance of my approach'!

I had identified what I called the exploitative network, comprising powerful economic-political interests in the rich countries and many of the elites in perhaps most of the poor ones. These combined to continue bleeding the EDCs of their wealth of raw materials. This not only did not help the poor, but made their condition yet more miserable. For example, the increased cultivation of cash crops, such as tea, coffee, cocoa, rubber to satisfy European or American markets often jeopardises the national economy through fluctuations in the world market. However, even when the product is fetching good prices, the poor still suffer. The peasant communities are deprived of land and hence of a good and varied diet, as well as being enslaved to a precarious economy and to rapacious employers and landlords. Thus the gap between the rich and the poor widens. This occurs not only between the wealthy and the impoverished nations but, within the latter, between the prosperous towns and elites on the one hand, and on the other hand the increasingly destitute rural areas and the vast new shanty towns, *bidonvilles* and *favelas*.

Most people were not unaware of these facts. However, they were obsessed by the theory that development was to do with increasing savings. These would make it possible to build more roads, factories, irrigation systems, hydro-electric plants and the like, which would in turn make it possible to build yet more roads, factories, etc. Eventually, with luck, more resources would be available for schools, hospitals, houses and so on which would raise the living standards of the people who had done 90 per cent of the work. This was called, as it is today, for some people still believe in it, the trickle down theory.

Now, having been involved in development efforts off and on for some forty years, it is clear to me that most of the poor are often poorer, more oppressed and, because these things hang together, hungrier, sicker and living more disrupted and unhappy lives. Most of this global deterioration has been brought about by the lethal impact of the greed of the rich nations whose economic stranglehold, often disguised as development aid, has in fact *de*developed those parts of the earth we have also variously called underdeveloped and developing; the word I have just used is far more truthful. It is abundantly clear that the wealth has not, in fact, trickled down. The channels down which it could have flowed to those most in need of it, have been effectively dammed by the political and economic depredations of the rich, who preferred to keep it for themselves by, for example, reduction of taxation for the rich and cutting expenditure on social services.

I realised that if development were to improve the lot of all the people, and I saw no other worthy purpose, no purely *economic* policy could bring it about. It could only occur in a milieu that was politically and morally favourable, one that would ensure the just distribution of advantages deriving from development and prevent them from draining away through corruption and through the demeaning and ultimately destructive conditions imposed by the donors of aid. In this last respect, I was greatly impressed by the approach of Julius Nyerere, struggling valiantly for the prosperity of his desperately poor country. He was well aware that countries may be offered a loan for something vital — say a fertiliser factory or an irrigation system for a country with chronic food shortages — and then be blackmailed into accepting ruinous and degrading conditions. They must pay it back at heavy interest; give very favourable concessions for timber or mineral extraction; use only the donors' carriers; employ only the donors' experts and technicians; buy only the donors' goods (at high cost) and sell their own raw materials (at low cost); agree to the establishment of military bases; and the like. All in all, such arrangements mean that the donors extract from the unfortunate recipient much more capital than they put into the factory or whatever they have supplied: a good investment indeed, one which has contributed to the ruination of the dedeveloped economies and the misery of the local peoples. Of this sort of exploitation Nyerere said that he would always reject it. Even if, improbably, it were financially sound, the subservience could only impair the dignity of his people — and that was the essence of development.

I began to think anew about development. Up to this point my chief interest had been in social development through improved education, health provision, and so on; but I had thought of these largely as a means towards an economic end. The attainment of this would then facilitate the creation of a more desirable society. A new class of educated and competent citizens would be able to enhance what was already admirable and eliminate what was not. But what was and what was not admirable? Few of the people I knew, except one or two committed ideologues, seemed to have considered the character and quality of the 'developed' society they were working to create — or if they had, they perhaps pictured something rather like their own.

Eight years after my *Educational Strategies* I wrote another called *Making Peace* in which I tried to define my new concept of a developed nation. The criteria were no longer economic, such as per capita gross national product and in fact not statistical at all but descriptive (educational, medical, nutritional, etc.). I maintained that the type of society we should try to work towards had the following characteristics:

Sufficiency. By this I meant that the standard of material provision of health care, food, shelter would ensure that no one was prevented from developing his or her personal potential through avoidable ill-health, ignorance or discomfort.

Security. This implies that there is a low level of violence, both physical and administrative, and that the individual is safeguarded from abuse from landlords, employers and officialdom; perhaps as a necessary condition for this, the individual must also have some part (unnecessary at this stage to define) in the political process.

Satisfaction. This means that life should offer pleasure and enjoyment. In particular Sufficiency should not be achieved at psychic or cultural cost (of anomie, alienation or family disruption) such as is suffered by those who migrate to lucrative jobs in grim urban factory conditions as I have seen in Pakistan and South Africa.

Stimulus. This emphasises the importance of growth and change. I would never advocate a smugly static society however prosperous. No such society could meet the challenging opportunities for creative development offered by the new technologies. It implies also the chance of the individual human being to grow to full stature throughout the right educational opportunities; while at the same time it also presupposes a social order which will permit and encourage each individual to take an appropriately constructive place within it.

If indices for the achievement of such a society are required they would be less related to the economy than to the condition of the mass of the people. Statistics relating to health, life expectancy, literacy, education, libraries, cultural amenities, participation in community and local government activities would all be revealing. In fact this sort of evaluation has become much more prevalent during the last two decades. However, at the same time that the well-being of the person has been given greater attention as compared with overall economic indices which showed nothing about it, the need for large scale and costly projects continues. Roads, hospitals, bridges, irrigation systems, factories, power stations, etc. must still be built if nations are to meet their obligations to their people. So the problems of development in the conventional form of economic development continue, and will continue, even if another concept of what true development means has superseded the one we started with.

Chapter Eighteen
Illustrative facts and figures ★

Although the global economy has grown considerably since 1960 (GNP will approximately have tripled by 1990) there has not, for the less favoured 70% of the population, been much change for the better; the wealth has not trickled down to them and some of them indeed are worse off. It is true that there was an average gain in income for the poorest fifth of $54 (all dollar values calculated in real terms), but the gain for the richest fifth was $4,224, while the gap between highest and lowest income levels doubled during this period. This applied within and between both rich and poor countries; for instance, 35m US citizens are below the poverty line.

Moreover, throughout the world, there are very few examples of the just, well-ordered society that I would consider truly 'developed'. In a world that possesses collectively both the resources and the technology to solve all its material problems it seems shameful and wasteful that so much of its population should be engulfed by violence, and is hungry, sick and oppressed. This situation has in many respects worsened during the last twenty five years. As for violence, some 70 new wars have been fought since 1960. In these the proportion of civilian deaths has risen from 52% in 1960 to 85% in 1980. Our age is indeed one of rampant militarism. Since 1945 military expenditure has quadrupled and now amounts to over $20 trillion (add twelve 0s), which is six times as large as the annual income of 3.8b people in the Third World.

The arms trade is a significant item of rich country economy amounting in 1986 to $2,736b. Most sales were to the Third World of which Africa's share in the same year was $5,730m to add to her general military budget of $15,154m; this last figure had risen from $8383 including arms purchases, in 1960 and may be compared with a total of $17,453m for health and education combined. The annual cost of a soldier has risen between 1960 and 1986 from $31,046 to $54,148 in 28 wealthy nations (in the U.S. the latter figure is $89,228) and from $2,854 to $10,200 in 113 poor ones.

Note that by contrast the average yearly educational expenditure per school child in the Third World in 1982 was $91: this seems a clear indication of priorities.

During the post war period, and particularly between 1960 and the present, when about two thirds of the world's nations gained independence from colonialism, there has been a proliferation of military regimes. In 1987 there were 49 in the Third World of which all but two were addicted to the most brutal of repressive measures — torture, political killing and 'disappearances'. Where such violence rules, development of any sort, except the further enrichment of the small ruling elites, is impossible.

Health and education expenditure have admittedly increased, but not proportionately to the need of the increasing population. Although there are actually more children in school, the number not in school is growing and there are, for example, 2m more illiterates every year. Today, 77m do not get enough food to lead a normal working life, 1,300m do not have safe water to drink, 800m exist in absolute poverty without enough to meet irreducible needs, 14m children die annually of famine-related diseases, and there are 12m refugees fleeing terror or famine at home.

Throughout most of the Third World the demands of the military, coupled with pressures of burgeoning populations for even the minimum care, mean that governments must sprint to stand still while the majority, save for the few oil rich, are falling behind, and depend on borrowing to survive. Now the increasing burden of debt drives them into forms of production, such as cash cropping, that ruin their people and drive them further into pawn to the donors. Add to this the ultimate effects of ecological devastation carried out by rich and poor alike that loom like monstrous ghosts through the mists of the near future. Top off this vision of the world with the nuclear Democlean sword that overhangs us all and our original thoughts of development, including mine of Sufficiency, Security and the rest, become childish dreams, laughable and best forgotten.

How did things come to this sorry pass? At the end of World War II it seemed that the shattered world was being reborn. We seemed to have both the means and the will to share our wealth (at least to some extent) and were driven by a newly acquired sense of responsibility for our less fortunate brethren. Even the speedy advent of the cold war did not stand in the way of development as we then conceived it. In fact, it became a spur as one or other of the protagonists sought to gain influence in the new nations. Bodies like the Food and Agriculture Organisation, the World Health Organisation and the United Nations International Children Fund did and are doing wonderful work. Private charities such as Oxfam and War on Want gave great service. So did a few national governments, such as those of Scandinavia and the Netherlands. Thousands of men and women worked and are working with skill and dedication in places where their abilities were needed. All this was new; but what went wrong? Why are 70% of the world's population now worse off than they were before this great effort began?

The random statistics I have presented suggest three things. The most striking is, perhaps, a universal obsession with militarism. I remember noting with dismay that one of the first things most newly independent nations yearned for was an air force, a macho symbol of their new status. The great spenders have been of course the super powers, though military budgets in the Third World have grown proportionately. But behind this fascination with armies and weapons lurks the poison of hatred closely allied with fear, the desire for revenge, the love of domination and anger against whomsoever would stand in the way of new found national identity.

The second element is woven around the poison of craving. This is related to greed, rapacity and acquisitiveness. It is clearly demonstrated by the way in which national governments give aid to the Third World. Apart from military aid which the donor often believes to be to his own strategic and of course economic advantage, the ever-richer rich countries feed relatively small quantities of aid into the poor ones. For example, between 1960 and the present there has been no increase, in real terms, in their aid-giving, whereas allowing for inflation, military expenditure rose by 80%. Moreover, such aid as is given is usually for purposes that will be of advantage to the donors, e.g.technical education that will provide staff for corporations based in their own countries. During the same period GNP per capita in the 28 rich nations has slightly more than doubled from $5,000 to $10,000 (in the U.S. $15,540).

It has also almost doubled in the Third World, but only reached $788. These figures strongly suggest not only a neglectful lack of care for the poor on the part of the rich but, as we have already seen, economic (and political) exploitation and domination. As we have contributed to their dedevelopment, we have grown fat on their deprivations. In our gluttonous rape of the Third World (which began centuries ago with the slave trade) we hardly realise that we have created both the environmental and the politico-economic problems and perils that are already with us or foreshadow the future.

The third element is ignorance. We hardly know what we are doing, so blinded are we by militaristic hatred and the craving for profit. Protected by deep-seated prejudice and racism, we hardly see that those we make suffer are human beings like ourselves. Below this level of ignorance is the deeper one — we do not know ourselves. We are unaware of our potential for perfection; failing to recognise this we are full of self-hatred which we turn outwards onto others, and glory in our military preparations to kill them. To these deluded feelings, we add the belief that we shall find happiness in external things, hence our grasping for wealth and power.

Before considering the nature of a form of society within which these poisons might be more easily contained and neutralised, and the even harder problem of how to get there from here, I should ask a question. Why should our affairs have become so desperate at a time when we might have anticipated an improvement?

The first part of the answer is that they would undoubtedly have been even worse had not a strong spirit of altruistic internationalism and of sensitivity to human suffering developed and persisted, especially after the world wars. Even more powerful, however, was the impetus of opportunity for profit opened up by the decline of empires coupled with astounding advances in technology and air travel. It must also be recalled that the countries of Europe especially were no strangers to exploitation and mercantilism; the financial mechanisms and expertise were all there, ready to swoop onto new prey.

Derived for the most part from Ruth Leger Sivard, *World Military and Social Expenditures*: 1987/8

World Priorities, 1987 and earlier volumes.

The sources are documents and reports of the United Nations special agencies, the World Bank and comparable institutions.

Chapter Nineteen
Cases

The brief studies that follow illustrate some of the intractable difficulties of development. Those who have worked in the field are invited to skip the next few pages, for they will all have too many examples of comparable situations.

The Afghan Powindahs

These are the Pushtun tribes which, in normal times, have always seasonally migrated at the beginning of winter from the bitterly cold mountains of Afghanistan to the somewhat more clement hills of western Pakistan, whence the young men would roam off (the word Powindah is related to the English 'wander') to trade and seek seasonal employment. The families would remain in the highlands with their camels, their goats, their fat-tailed sheep and their chickens. It was wonderful to meet these nomadic armies on the move with their caparisoned camels, their bright-clad women and their wolfishly handsome men.

They would remain during the winter months, grazing their animals and trading their dried fruits, nuts and skins for the luxuries that Pakistan had to offer. They would then return westwards in the spring. One day, however, during the period when I was advising the Pakistan government on social issues, including tribal ones, I was asked to make contact with the Powindahs to tell them that the Pakistani authorities no longer welcomed them in their country. The reason? Well, it seemed that the Afghan animals ate too much Pakistani grass and introduced diseases with which they infected the Pakistani animals. The Powindahs themselves similarly introduced diseases with which they infected Pakistani citizens, and what's more they were smugglers and thieves.

Consequently early one morning I set off with my two daughters, my Pakistani counterpart and a small posse of officials. We drove some distance from Quetta in jeeps, then transferred to horses and rode for several hours into the hills before arriving at the high valley where a large contingent of Powindahs were camped. The black felt tents were pitched at the far end of the valley and the hill sides were stippled with innumerable animals eating, of course, grass. As we neared the camp, two lines of young men came out to meet us and formed an avenue for us to pass through; as we did so, they let off volleys of shots. I am, to put it mildly, uneasy on horse back and it still amazes me that I stayed in the saddle.

Once in the tent we were feasted and treated to a display of dancing by the young men. They spun furiously around, long hair swirling, swords flashing and there was a great deal of shooting as the elders jumped from their seats beside us and let fly with their automatic weapons. Eventually we got down to business.

I reluctantly told our generous hosts what the Pakistani government had decreed: they must leave the country and not come back.

They looked sad and puzzled. Their spokesman said: 'We really don't understand these new things — Pakistan, Afghanistan, frontiers. What do they mean? All we know is that these mountains are our home and always have been.'

I rode back feeling very sorrowful, and determined to do what I could to plead the Powindahs' cause. But the government were implacable. The Ministry of Agriculture, they said, were insistent on the need to evict the Powindahs.

This, however, was not the end of things. When the Foreign Ministry heard what had happened, they in turn became insistent. It would be fatal, they said, because of the present alignment of power in Asia, to offend the Afghans. The parochial concerns of the agriculturists were overridden by a superior ministry and the Powindahs were allowed to stay.

But arrangements that depend on something so capricious as power politics can't be relied on to last. A few years later it became expedient to offend the Afghans in order to curry favour with someone else — I forget just whom — so the Powindahs, pawns in a deadly game, were pushed out once more.

And later still, after the Russian invasion, the Powindahs and indeed many more, came swarming back to the indirect benefit of the Pakistani government.

And who, in all this sorry story, thought of the needs of the Powindahs for support and development?

The Chakmas

These people are (or were) a Buddhist tribe of some 600,000 people, the largest group of the Chittagong Hill Tracts, formerly of East Pakistan, now of Bangladesh. They were a charming and highly artistic people and their society was gentle, peaceable and relatively prosperous in the fertile valleys between steep jungle-covered hills.

One day I discovered that a dam was to be built on the Karnafuli river (in fact it was halfway complete) and that the backed-up waters might flood out a few thousand tribal people. The purpose of the dam was to provide hydro-electric power for the coastal region, as well as to improve navigation and irrigation in the lower reaches of the river.

On visiting the region (and being captivated by the people) we found out that everything was much worse than anyone had realised at our end (the central government to which I was attached was located in West Pakistan, over 1000 miles away and no one knew or cared much about what happened in East Pakistan — still less if it happened to non-Muslim tribals). It turned out that the whole of the Chakma people would be made homeless and there was no suitable place for them to go; all their fruitful valleys would be flooded and there were no adequate alternative agricultural areas. But no one had done anything about all this, except that the provincial government had appointed one elderly clerk who was fumbling formalistically with insuperable problems of compensation.

I returned to Karachi, then the seat of government, full of anger and foreboding. I knew that plans for the dam could not be abandoned at this stage, but it should be possible to stir people up enough about the impending disaster for something to be done to soften it. Committees were set up and the East Pakistan government established the machinery for providing new (unsatisfactory) settlement sites, facilities for fishing industries on the sides of the vast lake that would be formed, advice on cultivating the hillsides, and so on.

Not long after, I left the country. Some eight years later, I asked a friend living in Dacca if he could find out what had happened to the Chakmas after the completion of the dam. Some of the things we had recommended, it turned out, had been done, but on the whole the condition of the Chakmas was deplorable. The new settlements were periodically flooded, the hillsides were useless compared with the lost valleys, the young people had drifted down to the coast they had hitherto shunned and had contracted TB and syphilis, the communities which were formerly close-knit in adjacent valleys had fragmented, the mood was hopeless and unhappy.

The final irony was that the dam hadn't worked. No one had realised that when the great monsoon rains — about the heaviest in the world — fell directly onto the lake surface, the water level would rise very much faster than when the water trickled down the innumerable hillside streamlets to the lake. The waters overflowed the dam, their force cracking it, silted up the irrigation works and the navigation channels; so no one had gained anything from it — except of course the contractors who had long since pocketed their profits and pushed off home!

Now, nearly twenty years on again, the dam is to some extent working, but the condition of the Chakmas has deteriorated even more. Their hostility to their provincial government, which they held responsible for all their woes, led some of them to support the West Pakistan army in the independence struggle of 1971. This apparently amounted to very little, but it served as an excuse to the authorities in newly founded Bangladesh to make inroads into the tribal territories. The Chakmas were evicted from much of the land they still held, to make way for Muslim settlers from other areas. Some tried desperately to resist and there have been terrible reprisals. Thousands of others have fled to India. The few who know and care about the situation speak sadly of genocide, not exactly in the sense that everyone has been killed, though many have, but that a nation has been destroyed.

Chitral

This is a semi-independent principality at the north-west tip of Pakistan. It lies beyond the Himalayas in the Hindu Kush mountains adjoining Afghanistan and the USSR. My wife and I approached it from Hunza in the high Karakoram and Gilgit and walked and rode for several days until we came to the Shandur Pass, a high windy plateau — a parmir — jewelled with lakes beside which grazed yak and dzo.

From the far side of the plateau we looked thousands of feet down to the minute settlement of Laspur crouched at the foot of a rotting glacier from Buni Zom, at 21,000 feet a relatively minor peak. When we had stumbled down to Laspur the men who had accompanied us on the previous stage dropped our luggage and hurried away with their animals, saying that these were bad people. Indeed, the appearance of the villagers was not too encouraging. They approached us with angry shouts as we sat and looked about us disconsolately; the village which had looked picturesque from far above was a collection of unpromising huts divided by rushing streams.

We managed, however, to put together enough of various languages to gather what they were saying in a mixture of Urdu and their own language, Quor. They were mortified, they said, that they could not feed us; they were starving themselves. We said, no matter, we weren't hungry (we hadn't eaten that day), but if they could find us somewhere to sleep and a couple of horses to go on with our journey next morning, we would be very happy.

They put us in a hut, and lit a fire, which was very generous as 12,000 feet up in the mountains there is very little fuel and they mostly used large dried leaves, rather like rhubarb. We were soon warm and comfortable — the huts are only about six feet high to conserve the heat, and all spend a happy evening together. I passed round cigarettes and we brewed a packet soup from Kashgar that we had picked up somewhere. It tasted revolting, but took the edge off the appetite.

As the evening passed, we pieced together some understanding of their circumstances. Their country had been invaded, some three hundred years ago, by the king of neighbouring Badakhstan, a descendant of Tamurlane, who had been forced to flee after a palace coup. He came with his entourage of nobles and they settled down and married the local Chitrali princesses, forming an elite caste known as the Adamzadas; our friends constituted a caste of semi-slaves known as the *faqir mishkin* — the miserably poor. They were called on for forced labour, keeping the tracks open (many of these were carved out of the mountain sides and constantly blocked by landslides and falls of rock), repairing the swinging bridges of willow withies, and working on the great castles of their overlords.

If they protested they were beaten or even shot; there was no redress. To top it all, they were taxed in kind — a tithe of their very limited crops.

High in the mountains grain is not easy to grow in sufficient quantities. Every year, after taxation, the previous harvest was exhausted before the new one was ready. Every year there was a period of about six weeks (in the middle of which we had arrived) when there was virtually no food. Grass seasoned with salt was the staple diet and the most common cause of death during these famine weeks was stomach blockage caused by the grass.

Was there nothing they could do about this, we asked? No, they answered; it had always been like this, the rich oppressed the poor and the poor suffered: there was nothing anyone could do about it; it was the will of God.

Across the mountains, a hundred or so miles away, were the socialist philosophies of Russia and China, but they might as well have been on the moon.

My brief for this trip had been to discover what was really happening in this remote and inaccessible region. Now that I had found out, what could I say? What forms of development activity could be of service to the unhappy Chitralis? It would not have been difficult to make constructive sounding suggestions, but what was the chance that they would be implemented under the autocratic rule of the Adamzadas? In any case, this was an acutely sensitive area, the meeting point of Russia, China, Afghanistan and Pakistan; the overriding geo-political considerations might affect any solution for the development problems of a few poor mountaineers; who cared about them anyway? I decided that the best thing I could do was simply to recount as graphically as possible what we had seen and learned; to point out that this was a source of potential unrest in a strategically significant zone, and to leave it at that.

I know that the situation has not remained unchanged, but have been unable to go back to discover the details.

The reader is invited to skip the next three pages as perhaps unrelated to the theme of development or, more properly, deprivation. I had at first decided to omit them, but rather reluctantly because they round off the story. Later, however, I decided to include them thinking they may not be entirely irrelevant since there can sometimes be a link between the pathology of individuals and of societies.

We set off before dawn on the following morning, moving like ghosts through the silent village. All day we walked down the valley with two of our friends to guide us and lead the horses with our luggage. We became very tired and hot, despite being cooled off by the many deep and icy streams we had to cross, and were relieved when, about ten hours later, we sighted our destination. This was the home of the powerful Adamzada family Khushwaqt. We could see it a long way off: a sort of castle surrounded by a vast mud wall which was strengthened by tree trunks, where the valley widened and the river we had been following all day flowed into another.

After parting from the generous villagers, we were shown into an orchard within the walls and greeted by a charming and handsome young man, who told us in adequate English that he was Humayun, son of Colonel Khushwaqt, the governor of the Northern Province, who unfortunately was away; but he would be happy to look after us instead.

We sat under the apple trees beside a streamlet, drinking tea and eating fried chapattis; our luck had changed, we thought. Humayun told us that he would arrange horses for us for the next stage of the journey, but that we must leave early, by five, because there was a long day's march ahead.

But later, over an excellent dinner, his manner changed. No longer courteous, he was first moodily abstracted. Then increasingly excited, he began to tell us the grisly history of what members of his family had done, not only to their enemies,but also to each other. We were treated to a sequence of horrible episodes — grandmothers poisoned, babies' brains bashed out, impalings, cousins suspended by their thumbs over slow fires, delicate and gradual cuttings up with sharp knives, butchery of trusting guests like ourselves. After each incident he pushed back his chair, laughing wildly and saying, with apparent approbation, 'we are a bloody people'. And that, as we already knew and later confirmed from many sources, was their reputation; the Adamzadas were notorious for cruelty and treachery laced with charm. We went sombrely to bed — and were kept awake most of the short night by myriad bedbugs lured from the joints of the wooden charpoys by the scent of warm flesh.

At five, however, we were the only people around. We had packed our luggage and taken it outside the great wall, hopefully waiting for horses, several of which we saw in a nearby field. We also hoped for breakfast, but no sign of that, either. After about two hours people began to turn up; around a dozen men with swords in their belts, dressed in a sort of rough uniform of sheep skins, and a polo band. Polo originated in these parts, a very rough game played on any patch of more or less level ground available amid these enormous mountains; many of the men we had met earlier played avidly. (Polo, I'm told, is the Tibetan for ball.) The band, composed of drums and woodwind like a cross between clarinet and oboe, plays an accompaniment to the game, the various tunes informing those too faraway to watch, about the state of play.

Then Humayun appeared. After the manic note on which the evening had ended, he was now once more sombre and laconic. No, he told us, there were — despite the visual evidence — no horses, there was no means of transportation. We wandered disconsolately around the castle wall and he followed, smirking to himself. The band started to perform, but I don't know what the music conveyed to the listeners who could interpret it.

Then our insane young host turned to his band of retainers. He giggled, grimaced and pointed to us. They drew their swords and advanced steadily, but, I felt, reluctantly towards us. We stood there, backs literally to the wall; Humayun sniggered and the wild music filled the valley.

We both felt he was intending to experiment with some of the tricks we had heard about the previous night. Anne whispered that the only way out was for me to shout at him like a colonel (his father, like many of the hill princes had done his stint in the Indian army learning how to fight his local enemies). I barked at him angrily and haughtily, and told him that we had had enough of this tomfoolery; he had better get us horses straight away, or it would be the worse for him. The effect was immediate. He almost shrivelled physically, and dismissed his men; within a quarter of an hour horses appeared and we left.

We rode hard for the next three days, somewhat afraid that he might recover a vengeful nerve and pursue us. But he didn't; all we had to contend with was hunger and tracks which in places were crumbling and less than two feet wide with a thousand feet to fall on one side and a gigantic mountain on the other. To make things very much worse, Anne developed a painful fever, and I helped her, swaying and almost unconscious, onto her horse.

Eventually, however, we safely reached the town of Chitral, the capital of the state. Antibiotics put Anne right and we rested for a couple of days. During this time, we heard that Humayun's father, the colonel, was in town to visit the Metah, as the ruler is called, then a six year old boy. We decided to visit him.

He seemed like a tough and jolly brigand. We told him we were sorry to have missed him when we passed by his home, but that his son had given us hospitality. He looked at us intently, and asked as it seemed to us, somewhat anxiously, 'Was it all right?'

'Oh, yes,' we said, 'it was fine'.

He let out his breath slowly. 'Good', he said. 'I'm very glad'.

Chapter Twenty
The Arusha Declaration

The most deliberate and systematic effort (at least of which I know) to plan national development on a not primarily economic basis was made by Julius Nyerere, who was first president of Tanzania and so remained most honourably for a quarter of a century. His approach to the subject is set out in the Arusha Declaration of 1966.

Nyerere is a serious Catholic and a socialist and his approach is based on what he terms 'African socialism'. The credo of this approach is :

1. That all human beings are equal;
2. That every human being has a right to dignity and respect;
3. That every citizen is an integral part of the nation, and has an equal part in government at local, regional and national government levels;
4. That every citizen has the right to freedom of expression, of movement, of religious belief and of association within the context of the law;
5. That every individual has the right to receive from society protection of his life and of property held according to law;
6. That every individual has the right to receive a just return for his labour;
7. That all citizens together possess all the natural resources of the country in trust for their descendants;
8. That in order to ensure economic justice the State must have effective control over the principal means of production; and
9. That it is the responsibility of the State to intervene actively in the economic life of the nation so as to ensure the well-being of all citizens and so as to prevent the exploitation of one person by another or one group by another, and so as to prevent the accumulation of wealth to an extent which is inconsistent with the existence of a classless society.

Four cardinal points of Tanzanian socialism are that there should be no class of persons living off the labour of others, except for such as children and the disabled; that major means of production are under the control, through their government, of the workers; that socialism cannot exist without genuine democracy; and that socialism is an ideology which can only work properly if believed in and practised fervently.

These perhaps philosophical points are given practical expression through the principle of *self-reliance,* with which the bulk of the Declaration is concerned. The country, it says, is engaged in a struggle against poverty and oppression, but is consistently using the wrong weapon — MONEY (it is thus capitalised to emphasise the point). But more money (for schools, roads, hospitals, etc.) means more taxes and so there is an incessant demand for loans, grants and private investment from abroad. It argues against reliance on support from abroad for two main reasons — that enough would never, in fact be forthcoming, and that it would not be given without strings which would strangle the country's independence, diminishing the dignity of the people which is the essence of development. Instead, there must be emphasis on hard work and the use of intelligence, coupled with a concentration on agriculture rather than industry. (Many newly independent Third World countries concentrated their efforts on industrialisation as a sort of symbol of emancipation and modernisation.)

There is much stress on human beings, their involvement in the processes of development, their hard work, their rejection of laziness and drunkenness, their good housing, their self-reliance. In the sphere of education, advancement to secondary education (not a universal privilege in this very poor country) will not only depend on scholastic ability, but also on social responsibility. This is largely demonstrated by children's active participation in the efforts of the primary school to make itself self-sufficient by growing its own food and where possible selling it.

Julius Nyerere and his TANU ruling party have not found it easy to implement this policy. Competitive materialism, as everywhere, has strong roots in the country and they grow deeper every time a poor African sees a rich one with a smart car or a refrigerator, or every time a rich African sees an even richer European. It could hardly be expected otherwise. Although Nyerere may have exhorted, he could not punish greed or selfishness — it would be to undermine the democracy he cherishes. Nevertheless it is a vitally important first step that one country is founded on principles which, if not in so many words, are directed against the three poisons.

Chapter Twenty One
Towards a Transformed Society

It seems to me inescapably clear that our civilisation, the dominant, domineering western model that controls the fate of the world, is desperately flawed by destructive and greedy institutions. Perhaps it was not always so, for it has had wonderful products, artistic, scientific, political and humanitarian, but these have been overshadowed by the rapacious violence it has generated to destroy both its own — and of course, without compunction, other — peoples, and now ultimately its own natural environment. We have loosed the controls that held the worst manifestations of the three poisons in check. These are now infecting us, our institutions and our world with a sickness that may prove fatal unless we learn to *behave differently*.

Let us make a leap of imagination and try to envisage a world in which the poisons were sufficiently abated for us to achieve the Sufficiency, Satisfaction, Security and Stimulus, and of course much more than these simplistically formulated goals, that I once proposed as genuine development. I now see no possibility of reaching anything by tinkering with the system we now possess; it has proved too vulnerable to abuse and corruption.

It may be objected that we do not have a really global system, only about 150 separate nation states. However, once we are talking of national rather than the tribal or other sub-national systems that are included in many of them, there is considerable uniformity. The dominant elements are nationalism and dedication to national sovereignty, centralised government with its armed forces and host of officials to do its bidding, and ministries dealing with various aspects of national life, as well as involvement in a network of international connections, economic, diplomatic, scientific and communicational. I have had dealings with a number of governments in all continents and always found their fundamental structure recognisable, even if the actual settings differed greatly and even if the component individuals had been nurtured in vastly differing cultures; moreover, the fact that governments were based on dissimilar ideologies by no means made them dissimilar in function and purpose.

But even if it is legitimate to generalise about larger political units, is it nevertheless futile to seek solutions to our present troubles through imaginary scenarios? I do not think so. If we set our minds on distant goals — and distance does not necessarily imply improbability — it will be easier to take realistic steps towards approaching them. So it was with the planning of a united Europe; what a few decades ago seemed an absurd mirage is now palpably becoming a reality (though not necessarily quite the reality I would advocate as the best way through the wilderness of our troubles). If, on the other hand, we reject images of the future we shall blunder around entangled in today's problems, seeking short-term palliatives for fundamental difficulties and never escaping from the conditions that created them. So it is good to be boldly imaginative. As we approach the distant mountains we may see a better route for climbing them than if we only view them from below. But if we never set out, we shall never climb them at all.

Democracy. This is the most potent political idea the world has ever seen It recognises that all human beings share in the same nature and that that nature is basically good and trustworthy, capable of making wise and humane decisions. Any system that excludes anyone from having a say in what matters to us all must, by the same token, be bad. Truly democratic governments are most praiseworthy, but many that call themselves democracies in fact have ways of excluding various categories of people from full participation in the processes of democracy — which cannot then be said to exist.

Equally, however, there are individuals who abuse their democratic privileges. They either do not vote, or are too ignorant of what is at stake to vote sensibly and with care, or they vote out of prejudice or self-interest without thought of what is best for the many — or indeed what 'the best' means. This greatly decreases the value of the system. A further abuse is that so many individuals seek election to office for 'I' reasons; for personal ego enhancement or (which of course is usually synonymous) material profit. Then again, in

certain systems, some when once elected may remain in office long
after their potential usefulness is past — as, for example, in the
recently collapsed Communist regime in the German Democratic
Republic. Age, boredom or loss of initial enthusiasm may diminish
effectiveness even if the attractions of office remain strong. In
addition, there are those who in one way or another, in extreme
cases by bribery or other malpractice, more commonly by clever
manoeuvring, have manipulated their election. Finally, some are
elected less because of any personal qualities than because they
represent a point of view (or a party) which is popular or is in one
way or another able to exert influence. Such flaws in the
functioning of democracy do much to impair its potential for
maintaining a society based on genuine recognition of unity and
worth of human, and indeed of all life. We have not been able to
obliterate hierarchy, privilege and inequality however well they may
be disguised. In the growth of our political systems, even the most
democratic ones, we have also created a seed bed for the
pullulation of the three poisons.

What follow are examples — and there may be many other and
better ones — of the sorts of conditions which might contribute to
establishing a genuinely *developed* society, a more effectively
democratic society.

I realise that all the suggestions that follow are capable of gross
abuse. The first two, for example, go contrary to the wise principle
of 'one man one vote' (which should of course be amended, if used,
to 'one person one vote'). But though protecting us against
domination by an elite, this principle also limits the initiative and
capacity for service of those who have much to contribute. There
are safeguards against abuse in clauses 3 and 4 below, but the
measures adumbrated in this section constitute a package of not
only constitutional, but also psychological and/or ideological
measures. They hang together as in fact do all the measures that
sustain any system: the motives, aspirations and values that sustain
any group whether it be family or state must to a sufficient extent
reflect and be reflected in its governmental and other institutions. If
they do not, the group concerned will sicken and eventually fall
apart. This was the root of the failure of Communist regimes in
Czechoslovakia, Rumania and other European countries; the

behaviour and attitudes of those in power were completely discordant with the ideals of a classless and egalitarian society. The secret of democratic development is the creation and maintenance of harmony between a generous attitude towards all life and the structures required to provide for our material and social needs. It must be possible to move towards this goal from many directions:

1. Everyone over a fairly young age would be permitted to vote for their representatives for different offices. According to various criteria they would be allowed from, say, one to five votes .
2. The number of votes that might be cast by each individual in any given election would be determined by members of the community (a manageable unit which would need to be defined) according to age, education (see our later discussion — I am not referring to merely formal qualifications), sense of responsibility and contribution in the widest sense to the community.
3. Candidates putting themselves forward for election would be automatically disqualified. Instead, all would have to be nominated by the electorate. Like Roman consuls, African chiefs, or the Speaker of the British House of Commons, there would have to be reluctance — in this case adjudged genuine rather than symbolic — to stand for office, on the part of those selected.
4. Persons elected would only serve for a limited time (say five years) after which they would be released unless expressly requested to serve longer by their constituents.
5. Party politics, as we understand the concept, would cease to exist. They would be replaced by No-Party politics, to be discussed below.

No-Party Politics: This is not to be confused with the One Party systems of some communist countries, which is rule by the oligarchy of the party and not democratic at all — except in name.

Nor is it to be compared with the One Party systems of a number of African states, although there is enough in common with some of the underlying ideology to justify a brief discussion of them. When the mass of African nations became independent between the late 1950s and 1970, their departing colonial rulers bequeathed western-type constitutions allowing for multi-party legislature, drawn up by British, French, etc. lawyers. These were eagerly adopted as symbols of the modernisation for which they craved. However, within a few years they were almost all abandoned. One reason was that the political parties that arose were based less on different ideas of how to govern the country concerned, than on tribal affiliation: the legislative assembly simply became an arena for tribal conflict. There was, however, a deeper issue.

Many of the African peoples, particularly in West Africa, believe that there can be only one right way of responding to issues that affect the well-being of the community. There may be fierce argument as to what this way is, but eventually everyone comes to the same view. It is one of the functions of chiefs to bring this about. When they are acting in their chiefly role seated on the sacred Stool they act as a sort of lightning rod for the wisdom of the ancestors; and they are elected for their capacity to play this part. Thus they are able to guide, to ensure the continuity and relevance of the debate among the members of the tribe qualified by age or status, but not to direct it. This in some cases might include all adults. The discussion may last for hours, even days, but eventually all will reach the same conclusion; there cannot, after all, be alternatives to the truth.

Even though many may not now believe in the supernatural role of chiefs, there would appear still to be a deep-seated feeling that there cannot legitimately be more than one approach to the solution of political or social problems. A political system that allows for two or more parties with the right to propound different, even mutually exclusive programmes or views of national objectives, cannot be relied on.

A perhaps better known approach to the solution of problems and to decision-making on policy, is the Quaker business meeting. This, like the African tribal debate takes place within a spiritual context. In the Quaker case, the business meeting is also a meeting for worship. It is believed that if people come together with the right attitude, seeking the guidance of the Spirit within, the best course of action will eventually be revealed to all; a consensus — the 'sense of the meeting' — will be reached. This does not, however, preclude a lively debate. Indeed a debate, if carried out and listened to seriously and sensitively, is an important part of reaching what is ultimately accepted as the right answer. Two further points about Quaker democracy may be noted: all Members of the Society of Friends (and often many who are not actually Members, but regular Attenders) may take part in many business meetings — since decisions are reached by consensus there is no question of who does or does not have voting rights; no votes are cast. Nor does anyone stand for election to the various offices and committees; they are nominated by a committee selected for the purpose. Once appointed, they serve only for a specified time; at the end of this period, the appointment may be renewed, but not indefinitely.

The No-Party systems of the African tribe (less so, at present, of the nation) and the Quakers have this in common: in no sense do they require uniformity of opinion or unanimity of outlook, no grim orthodoxy. They foster diversity and that diversity brings to the process of decision-making a remarkable depth and richness. The conclusion is not reached because it conforms to a particular ideology or school — say Leninism or monetarism — but through searching enquiry. But there is, at least among the Quakers, a common view of essentials (I would not try to generalise about the Africans). This is that the right policy (if that is not too formal a word) is one which promotes the full development of human potential, the happiness and well-being without discrimination of all women and men in a just, peaceful and completely non-violent world. How to work best towards this goal would depend upon varying circumstances, and about this there would be, and indeed is, continual debate — for situations change continually and cultural differences must be taken into account. However, the broad character of the objective would preclude all solutions that included violence towards any one, or which favoured any particular group at the expense of another, or which was not agreed to democratically.

And such would be, at any level, the basis of No-Party politics.

Universal Provisions of the No-Party system. Although this system is open, innovative and flexible, its basic principles just identified would require certain conditions for their fulfillment:

1. There would need to be a structure of regulatory bodies at various levels from the global to the regional and eventually down to local. In one sense this exists embryonically today with the global United Nations and its various agencies, regional bodies such as the OAU and the EEC, national governments, and county, town and even parish councils below them, each with differing degrees of autonomy. However, the most fruitful co-operation is jeopardised by concepts of sovereignty at the national level; this must be superseded by the concept of one world and universal citizenship.

2. Most wars and other intense conflicts are today not international but internal, between governments and groups which for racial, religious, linguistic or other reasons feel disadvantaged or oppressed. It would be important that the structure of regulatory bodies should eliminate such stressful relationships, e.g. the Kurds should no longer in any fashion be under the sway of Turks, Iraqis or Iranians.

3. Since peace is a prime concern of No-Party government, complete disarmament is an essential policy. The global and the regional authorities would, however, have access to a limited quantity of light arms for use in emergencies. Normally order would be maintained by unarmed police.

4. Many of our troubles stem from greed and from the inequalities which are engendered by its pursuit. Two measures may be suggested among many possible, for minimising the effects of this poison. One would be the introduction of a uniform rate of pay for politicians, professors, plumbers and paupers, but with special allowances for those doing dangerous, boring, unpleasant, highly responsible or stressful work, or having unusual personal commitments. The second would be for a tax structure that made the accumulation of vast fortunes virtually impossible. In the early days of Islam, the 'religious tax' of Zakat was devised for this purpose; it was to be paid directly to the poor, thus having the additional advantage of reminding the individual of his social responsibilities; the prohibition on charging interest had a similar purpose to that of Zakat.

5. A further source of injustice and conflict is the maldistribution of resources between individuals, states and whole areas of the world. One of the prime tasks of the various regulatory bodies would necessarily be to devise an equitable method of sharing the vast and varied resources of the world — not only of raw and manufactured material, but of human skills — technical, scientific, educational, artistic and managerial. Such a redistribution would enormously facilitate 'development' in the sense of sufficiency in food, health care, housing, communications, education, opportunity to participate in the arts — and so on and so on. We have today, indeed, all the resources needed for the nourishment and greatly improved health of the world's entire population. All that is needed is the ability and above all the will to distribute it equitably. The problems of development, however we understand the word, lie primarily in this area rather than in economics, agrimony, etc. (although there remains much work to be done in this field, particularly in reducing pollution in agriculture and industry). It is for this reason that this part of the book, entitled 'Development', is concerned more with the character and structure of human society than with such issues as economic growth.

It should be stressed that the suggestions made in this section are not prescriptions. The effects they are designed to achieve could no doubt be achieved by other and quite likely more appropriate means. They are, however, examples of how eventually — and after who knows after how much travail — we might overcome the flaws that mar our civilisation: the failure to achieve true democracy between nations and within them (my own country of Britain being an increasingly sad example); the persistence and in many areas the growth of inequalities between and within the nations of the world, and the associated failure to achieve development in the conventional sense of material sufficiency for all; the facile resort to violence to resolve differences; extremes of nationalism and tribalism that divide us and set us against each other.

Chapter Twenty Two
Towards a Global Identity.

Are all these suggestions absurdly fanciful and impracticable? No, they are certainly not. Throughout history what would have seemed unthinkable a few generations, or even a few years previously has happened. Consider the tremendous changes of the period of renaissance and reformation following the middle ages, the altered maps of Europe after both world wars, the rise of the welfare state in Britain after World War II, the fall of the great civilisations of antiquity and of the medieval African kingdoms of Mali, Songhai, Ghana and Zimbabwe, the transformation of Arabia, first by Ibn Saud and then by oil, the 'democratisation' of Japan after 1945, the 'economic miracles' of Hong Kong, Singapore and Taiwan during the last twenty or thirty years, the rise of the European community, the penetration of western thought by eastern philosophy during the last thirty years, the new ecological awareness introduced by Rachel Carson's *Silent Spring, glasnost* and *perestroika* in the USSR and the recent sudden eruption of democracy in Eastern Europe. All these and countless other 'unthinkable' things, good and bad, have happened. They were not in fact unthinkable; it was just that most people had lacked the imagination to think *about* them.

This is not to say, of course, that they will come easily. They *should* be thought about, carefully considered and worked towards to ensure that they take place as soon, as smoothly and as widely spread as possible. There is great value in planning change, but flexibly because such things never work out exactly as intended or predicted — I recall that when I worked with the Pakistan Planning Commission, there had to be six-monthly revisions of what was intended to be a five year plan because the circumstances in which the plan had been first drafted were not static.

I suppose it is hardly necessary to add that a change of constitutional or administrative arrangement does not guarantee the congruent change of heart that produces the desired result in a changed society. There must also be an evolution of attitude — hence the overwhelming importance of education in the broadest sense, which will be considered later. Nevertheless, it is safe to make two assumptions: that external change never begins at all unless changes in internal goals and perceptions have to some extent already occurred; and that external changes always affect attitudes. Everything that happens, in fact, results from the interaction of factors on all levels. Some measure of control over this interaction is the key to purposeful social change.

Attitudes towards wealth, power and social responsibility are central to this change. On the whole, opportunity accompanied by a certain modicum of challenge stimulates motivation. When wealth and power are available, those to whose 'I's they are desirable will strive for them greedily and energetically. But when they are not, when sufficiency rather than satiety is the attainable goal, the acquisitive motive is apt to be sharply reduced. The same is true of power. What I have suggested is a tax and wage structure that would minimise the possibility of any individual amassing a vast fortune, or of reaching a position of entrenched and unassailable political power. At the same time the electoral role of all citizens would ensure them a far greater quantum of social and political responsibility than ever before, perhaps, in modern society.

This, surely, would appeal strongly to everything in our real nature which is based on a sense of human — indeed living — unity and collective worth. By the same token it would help us to reject the delusions of independent self-sufficiency and the belief that we gain happiness from external rather than internal sources.

Chapter Twenty Three
Acting Ourselves

Ingenious people are always devising solutions to difficult problems. At least, they have done so for the ones I have been involved with. For example, during my years of concern over Northern Ireland, a new set of answers has been produced by somebody or other every few months. My usual response is one of surprised admiration; how brilliant, this might well work — I wonder why nobody thought of it before. But then, almost always, it doesn't work. The reason is the gap between the idea and its implementation; there is no direct channel through which the energy and ingenuity of the plan can pass to those who should implement it.

I do not want what I have proposed to become stuck in the same mud of inertia. In order for this not to happen anyone who favours the ideas propounded in the preceding pages must be *able to do something to put them into practice in however small a way*.

Because this is, or seems to be impossible in so many cases, the bright ideas are lost. People don't know what to do about them and so eventually they relapse into frustrated apathy. (This does not always happen, of course; the ideas of Marx, for example, were most vigorously put into action). One of the problems, I believe, is that the political and economic forces that dominate our world today are so powerful, so ubiquitous and so *universal*, that it is hard for us not to feel impotent before them. What can *we* do? What can we *do*? And the answer may well be 'nothing'.

But we must not allow ourselves to be brow beaten by the world of delusion. We have inner resources and capacities for strength, creativity and influence that command more authority than all the armies, stock exchanges and intelligence services in the world. This is not just me being fanciful; the great Mahatma Gandhi often affirmed that what he referred to as 'soul force' was the most powerful force in the world.

But even if we are not Gandhis (yet, but we can all move in the right direction), we can cultivate our soul force — in Tibetan terms, liberate the Buddha nature from the shroud of illusion and so greatly enhance our ability both to see and to act. We must have faith in ourselves, not the trumpery 'I' with its whims and vanities, fears and sense of inadequacy, but the ultimate reality of which we are the expression. To the extent that we do this, we shall recognise that there is always something we can do. To do this something we have to avoid the trap of thinking that unless we can solve one of the monstrous problems — famine in the Third World, the nuclear menace, environmental degradation, the decay of swollen inner cities — about which we know we can do virtually nothing, it is not worthwhile attempting anything else.

It is essential to remember that we are connected with everyone else. The legend of Indra's heaven tells that it contains an endless net and that at each intersection of this net there is a bead representing a life; each bead reflects and is reflected by every other. So it is with us. Every time, for example, that I buy a packet of coffee the life of a peasant in Columbia or Brazil is affected; likewise every time I refrain because my tastes have changed, or because the price has gone up. It would be an interesting exercise to go through our normal breakfast menu, especially the one called an 'English' breakfast to see how many other lives and peoples it touches — the bread, marmalade, bacon, milk, eggs, etc. etc. etc., will affect the livelihood and living standards of countless people. If we are in a bad mood at breakfast, our children or spouse will react during the ensuing day in a manner that will have some impact on the people they meet at school, at work, or even quite casually in shops or bus queues. Similarly, if we are cheerful, there will also be an impact, but of course a different one. Quite unwittingly, we affect not only the lives about us with which we have a recognised relationship, but also an infinity of others.

The vast and complex relationships of international diplomacy or trade with all their cross-currents of suspicion, anxiety, ambition and hatred are built on a foundation of trillions of breakfast-time relationships. We contribute to the scene we wish to change; we are not outside it, we are in it and part of it. Once we really recognise this fact, we become more aware of ourselves and the meaning of our existence as nodal points in the net of humanity.

If we bear in mind the ideal of *peaceful*, as opposed to unpeaceful

relations, we can make a serious effort to transform the ones we are
involved with and thus directly or indirectly, affect many others.

I can imagine that the reader may at this point say irritably that
this is all very well; it sounds very nice in a quasi-mystical fashion,
but just what does it do to slow down the arms race? Obviously I
don't know the answer, which will be different for every human
being depending what s/he does, meets, works at, where s/he lives,
his/her tastes, and so on. I can only say that the more aware we
become, the more we see opportunities (which were probably
always there) to do what contributes to harmony. Having done it,
we may never know who, as a consequence, does what next. We
can only be sure that the ripples from our actions will eventually
break upon the shores of eternity.

It is sometimes possible however, to be a little more definite. In
our state of relatively greater awareness we may spot unexpected
chances of more direct involvement in some major issue. But here
again a word of caution; in our concern over, for example, world
peace, we are dealing with enormous complexes of happenings on
every scale from the psychological to the geopolitical, from the
cellular to the wheelings and dealings of Wall Street, from the
pesticidal to the thermo-nuclear. Our fragment of the network of
relations may be relationships between toddlers in a nursery school,
or neighbours in adjoining allotments, or partners in a firm, or
vicars and curates, or council members and their constituents.
Never mind; these things all in varying degree add to the reservoir
of constructive compassion in the universe, or conversely to the
flickering mirage of fear and loathing — much depends on our
contribution, and our contribution depends upon our perception of
reality.

It would perhaps be easier to say we should become vegetarian,
join the Green party, study Tibetan Buddhism, be more generous to
Oxfam or Greenpeace, educate our children at home, go to a
homeopathic doctor, adopt a child of another race, and so on and so
on and so on. But prescriptions of this sort are worthless. Each
individual has to do what seems right and we can only make a
judgement on this when we have so far as possible cleared our minds
of illusion. We may then quite legitimately decide to do any of these
things — or indeed to stop doing them. What matters is that we

remain on the path to enlightenment and that we do all we can to develop more strongly within ourselves the motive of compassion towards all sentient beings.

It is also important that whatever we do, we should do well. So-called 'hard nosed' people in the 'real world' are apt to sneer at what they would call sentimental or impractical dreamers (like, I suppose, myself) and no doubt we sometimes merit that description. But this is a great mistake. The work, whatever it may turn out to be, we are attempting to do towards the transformation of the world is hard and difficult. It is all the harder for going against the current of conventional practice, often earning scorn and disapproval of those who follow the respectable tracks of illusion, especially those that extol the value and importance of material success. We owe it to our work to be as skilled and professional — perhaps, since the standards are not the usual ones, meta-professional — as the most hard boiled materialist.

The next two short sections suggest aproaches which may help towards transformational social change.

Chapter Twenty Four
Community Development

Community Development (CD) is an approach to helping communities to assume responsibility for their growth and change, and for shaping their own future. It is a process of empowerment that stimulates and leads out their capacities for initiative and independence. It is particularly valuable when these have been sapped by repressive traditions, unprogressive landlords and other authorities or, of course, by political oppressors. In those circumstances where mediation is impossible because a dominant power is fully convinced of his ability to crush a weak opposition, it is a means by which that opposition can gain sufficient strength effectively to challenge the rulers. These may eventually recognise the chance of defeat and so begin to consider the possibility of diplomatic solutions by mediation and negotiation, rather than continued violence. The principle of CD is to stimulate the self-confidence of a community, and faith in its ability (initially with help) to recognise and then to meet its particular needs.

We are all prone to a sense of guilt and worthlessness, both as individuals because of a faulty view of our own nature and as communities for the additional reason that those above us in the hierarchy of wealth, power and education have made us feel inferior and foolish by their contemptuous foisting of inferior roles and menial tasks upon us.

One of the greatest community developers I know is a former member of the Indian (and now the Pakistan) Civil Service (CSP), bodies not known for their egalitarian tolerance. But he thoroughly identified himself with the poor, and especially with the Bhils. These are a tribal people to whom he hoped to restore the pride in their culture that would enable them to improve their material state which had miserably lapsed because of apathy induced by unhappiness. Their pride and energy had been sapped by, among of course other things, ridicule poured on them by non-tribal neighbours for a rather peculiar reason: whereas westerners use paper for intimate personal hygiene, many others water, some sticks, the Bhil employ stones. When my friend met one in the forest and enquired who he was, he would hang his head and admit sadly, 'I am a Bhil; I use stones'. My friend, however, persuaded them that this was a cause for pride rather than shame. 'What is water', he said to them. 'It flows away and evaporates in the sun; or paper, the flames consume it; or sticks, they break and rot; but stones — they are everlasting even as the Bhil people'. He incorporated this theme into a song having the chorus 'We are Bhils; we use stones'. Before long the general level of their standard of living had been greatly raised.

I have seen CD in action, and had some slight responsibility for it, in many parts of the world, principally in Bangladesh and Pakistan in the very varied settings of rich agricultural areas of Punjab, the much poorer ones of Sind, the Tibetan-speaking villages of the Karakoram range, the remote settlements of Baluchistan, and the Pathan tribal areas of the north west frontier. The results on the whole were startling. People were doing what they had never done before; they were collaborating to keep their settlements clean, to buy seeds — or sometimes even a bull, — collectively, to construct community centres together, or dams or reservoirs or irrigation systems. The Village Agricultural and Industrial organisation (V-AID, as the CD organisation was called) was run by the government through its officials, presided over by a senior civil servant in each large administrative area. These, who had been brought up in the autocratic and elitist atmosphere of the CSP, might have been expected to dislike the increasing independence of a peasantry who had been little better off than serfs, but they became enthusiastic about this new phenomenon. One told me that not long ago, he had shouted angrily at a village cultivator who, while talking to him, had rested his hand on his, the official's, jeep. Now he shook his head in shocked wonder: 'How could I have done that?' he asked.

The village level workers were not, of course, gazetted members of the civil service. They were young women and men usually from the rural areas, who had had some training and then been dispatched, normally to areas with which they had some familiarity. They might easily have been rejected by the village elders, the panchayat, for their youth or because they came from the district and had no stranger value. But somehow they struck the spark. They led the villagers, encouraging them to identify their needs and hopes, until constraints of fear and inferiority had been broken and the villagers needed no more leading. In a fundamentally feudal and repressive society where landlords by right of custom if not law, have virtual power over life and death, this seemed to me and to others a first small breath of hope.

Then, suddenly, the whole thing came to an end. There were several rather implausible theories, but no one seemed really to know, or if they did they weren't saying, why something so successful had come to an end. But my friend, the Bhils' champion, had no doubts.

'The people were getting too much power', he said. 'They were beginning to think for themselves and work for themselves. Where would it end? The great landowners of Punjab and Sind, and don't forget they are also the great industrialists and the great ministers, they didn't like it. So — fooo — they blew the flame out'.

In Northern Ireland between 1970 and 1972 there was a government sponsored CD programme designed to counteract the impact of violence in shattering and dispersing the communities. Brave and idealistic young women and men from both communities and a few from mainland Britain were recruited and trained for the work.   Before long, however, this also was too successful. In turbulent conditions the authorities find that budding and critical democracies are less easy to handle than populations that are too frightened and confused to be anything but compliant. (The South African government found this also in Cross Roads, as have many tyrants.) An additional reason is thought to be that efforts to prevent mixed communities from splitting up were not welcomed by the army. They preferred to deal with clearly defined and separate Catholic and Protestant areas.

So it is precisely when CD is most needed that it is most likely to terminated by the authorities — or at least to be assailed.

This is perhaps the strongest proof that it is a powerful tool for liberation. Indeed, even before the authorities grasp what is really happening and act against it, an almost indestructible seed may have been sown and begun to germinate.

When I first encountered CD over 30 years ago I was deeply struck by its successes which, I thought, went beyond all bounds of reasonable expectation. Why did it almost universally flourish under circumstances which were extremely diverse and often largely unpromising? Now it seems to me clear that this can be attributed to the fact that it appeals to deep and indestructible features of our nature — genuine community with all others, coupled with unlimited capacity for achievement in fields in which we had believed ourselves to be ignorant or incapable.

Chapter Twenty Five
Non-violence

I regret using this negative term for something extremely positive. It is like saying non-hate instead of love! However, it is now widely known and understood and it would only cause confusion if I employed another word.

It still needs some specific definition, however. By non-violence I mean firstly achieving without harm to ourselves or others, things that are normally thought to be attainable only through violence. Secondly I mean the expression of *ahimsa,* what Gandhi called soul-force, to achieve these goals and thus to benefit not only ourselves but also those whose actions or policies we oppose. This also means loving our enemies, in fact not thinking of anyone as an *enemy.*

Non-violence is both an attitude and an action, but the latter will vary greatly according to circumstances.

The attitude, as I understand it, is one of taking from one group of people the pains of suffering from oppression and injustice; and from another the corroding burden of inflicting those hurts. Fundamentally it is an attitude of love.

The action may of course, be highly political. It may use many tools not only of persuasion but of coercion. These may include such economic weapons as strikes, boycotts, and even non-dangerous forms of industrial or other economic sabotage in order to force recalcitrant authorities to alter their policies. In addition there are the 'gentle' methods of what has been called mental jujitsu — ways of presenting the oppressor with the evidence of what he is bringing upon himself, what he is *really* visiting upon others.

But surely, it may be argued, this is really violent. What of economic sanctions (in South Africa or elsewhere) that deprive some of their wealth and possessions? Leaving out the complex arguments about possible effectiveness of economic sanctions and their impact on those who are already poor and deprived, let us consider the state of those newly deprived by the sanctions or other economic non-violent action.

Their state was previously most unhappy. Those who live fatly and with contentment on the misery of others must delude themselves most deeply to avoid being torn to pieces by guilt. They must desensitise conscience and sympathy with suffering to an extent that distorts and diminishes their whole being. In addition, they very often live in fear of the violence evoked by their callous disregard. They, even more than those they make to suffer, are the victims of their own materialistic greed, the poison that is maiming them. On the contrary, much good can be done and their natures even transformed if they can be helped to understand, through being forced to share more evenly (and not necessarily at great loss — the remaining white Zimbabweans have suffered little) the damage done by their selfishness.

But everything depends upon the compassion of the non-violent activists. If they are angry and embittered, then whatever they may do will only also evoke anger and bitterness. This would lead, as so often in the past, to a betrayal of a revolution. What had been initiated to restore justice and harmony spawns the opposite. The awareness and inner discipline of non-violent activists must be cultivated as diligently as their techniques of achieving social change.

These somewhat extreme measures should only be resorted to where the regular methods of democracy have failed to alter policies which were damaging to all members of the society except those who planned and implemented them. It is in general dangerous, in an operating democracy, to break the law even for plausible reasons. Only when it becomes inescapably apparent that government by the people no longer in fact exists and that terrible injustices are being perpetrated in their name, are such steps legitimate.

It is not uncommon for more militant social activists to be scornful of non-violence as a soft option. One misconception is that it involves little more than writing letters to the papers or to members of parliament, joining protest marches, making speeches, attending meetings — and in the evenings going comfortably home. For many, indeed, there is little beyond these innocent and not unuseful activities. But for the committed activist to embark on a non-violent campaign is like joining an army. It will demand a soldier's discipline, courage, and readiness to face hardship and danger for months on end. More, indeed. Guns give one a spurious self-confidence and it is far easier to face danger with a weapon in one's hand than without. But the non-violent forces are completely unarmed except with weapons of the spirit. They are the shock troops to be called upon when all chances of peaceful and positive development are fading.

It is perhaps appropriate to add a short note on the effectiveness of non-violent action. The story of Gandhi and the independence of India is, of course, well known. He must always remain the exemplar of the non-violent warrior, if such a term is permissible. His combination of spiritual insight and political acumen were phenomenal and his skills were in some measure passed on to Martin Luther King, Cesar Chavez and other activists who used with them with great effect. More recent examples, however, have received little attention. Perhaps the most dramatic of these was the Iranian revolution of 1968 when almost entirely unarmed mobs brought the state machine with its powerful army to a standstill, strangled the economy and forced the Shah and his government into exile. It is obviously true that the Iranian revolutionaries were not Gandhian in spirit. They would have had no objection to using guns if they had possessed them. But they did not, and faced the army to die in their hundreds — and the military, in admiration and remorse, joined them. To a somewhat lesser extent the revolutions in Haiti and the Philippines demonstrated that massive non-violence is an immensely powerful force. The revolution may not have lasted as — it seems — in Haiti, or be failing, as perhaps in the Philippines, or become itself extremely violent, as in Iran. This, however, by no means proves that the *tactic* of non-violence, even if divorced from its Gandhian spiritual ideology, is not exceptionally potent.

Indeed, since I drafted the previous paragraphs, amazing and encouraging examples of the 'soul force' of non-violence (coupled in varying degrees with not particularly Gandhian pressure) have been manifested in Eastern Europe.

I should, however, include a note of caution. Although the non-violent revolution may succeed, in the sense that it brings about the fall of a tyrannical regime, it may not succeed in the other sense of establishing one that is just and stable, or one whose justice and stability can withstand the harsh assault of circumstances. The political wisdom of the revolutionaries may not equal their non-violent ardour. There are signs that this may be the case in some areas of Europe whose revolutions are developing even as I write. All the more need, therefore, to follow the example of Gandhi, in seeking to complement the spiritual with the practical dimensions of non-violence.

Chapter Twenty Six
Conclusion

To complete this discussion of development, I should make explicit what I am sure has been observed as implicit throughout. This is, that the goal of development is developed people. Without women and men whose potentialities have been in some measure realised, no community of human beings can create and maintain the social structures and material conditions that provide lasting satisfaction to their members. At one level this is obviously a matter of cultivating the skills needed to support an adequate economy. At another, it depends on creating effective and equitable legal and administrative systems, and methods of control that are both just and efficient. At yet a third level it requires that the population are sufficiently motivated by values of social service and concern for the well-being of their fellows at home and abroad.

I particularly stress the latter, because if the values and aspirations of the people are flawed, the most perfect institutions will become tools for their personal purposes. But of course the two are interconnected, for if the institutions themselves are and can easily be put to corrupt uses, it is harder for people to resist the opportunity for dishonest gain. Nevertheless, mind is the source of our perceptions and desires; it imposes worth upon the things for which we crave. Although our normal perception of relative reality is dualistic, separating what is material from what is mental or immaterial, what is desirable and what is not, ultimate reality does not recognise these distinctions; everything is one, as our transformed nature will recognise.

It is for this reason that education, as we shall consider in Part III is crucial. If properly practised, it provides the skills to achieve the material goals of development and to ease the types of suffering caused by poverty and oppression. Even more importantly it can inculcate the attitudes of mind which make us less susceptible to these sources of anguish and more compassionate when we find them in others. We must acquire and impart the abilities and technical knowledge to achieve sufficiency, safety, and the rest. But these will only come in full measure when we have eliminated our faulty vision of reality; this alone will enable us to oppose effectively the three poisons which are the prime enemies of development by whatever criterion we define it. In the final analysis, a developed society can only be created and maintained by developed people who understand the truth of their own nature.

Chapter Twenty Seven
A Note on the Environment

When I first worked in the area of development, virtually nobody spared a thought for the environment — it was something to be used, not cared for. Rachel Carson's book was not published for some years after I became involved with the Third World, and although it made a deep impression, neither my colleagues nor I recognised its relevance for our own work. We blithely continued to build factories that belched poisons into the air, to clear away the forests, to spray pesticides with abandon, to build vast dams that destroyed communities and flooded good farm land, to cover more and more of the earth with tarmac for roads and airstrips, to ruin the soil with fertilisers that created dust bowls for the future.

It is true that the developers cannot be blamed for all the perils which we now recognise with alarmed clarity — the greenhouse effect, the damaged ozone layer, the depredations of acid rain, the questionable substances — some intended, some not — in our food, the almost universal pollution of our planet. Nevertheless we, with our limited philosophies, were not faultless.

We were, of course, ignorant. We were not aware of the possible consequences of policies and practices carried out mainly in good faith. Very often we were simply trying to do for the Third World what seemed to have been good for the rich nations: we wanted them, too, to enjoy the fruits of wealth.

But more crucial was ignorance not of practical matters, but of our own nature and potentiality. This leads to the illusion that happiness is the product of external factors, and so is the source of the other mutually reinforcing poisons of greed and dislike or hatred. (This is discussed at greater length in the Appendices 'Who Am I?' and 'The Three Poisons'.)

There is certainly an element of altruism in development and indeed generally in the production and provision of goods and services. But there is another one which is deeply flawed by grasping acquisitiveness and suspicious enmity towards possible enemies or competitors. These qualities inhere in the great commercial and industrial enterprises, in transnational corporations seeking profit at the expense of rivals, in national governments obsessed with sovereignty and preeminence.

There are of course noble exceptions, as there are among human beings. However, in general the ignorance of individuals — the false sense of self-existence, separateness, loneliness — tends to be writ large in the life of institutions, including those involved in planning and development. It is no wonder that the farmer will sacrifice the future health of his land for the sake of profit today, or that the nation will reject calls to restrict profitable industries whose toxic pollutants mostly affect the lakes and forests of other neighbouring countries.

Now, it seems, the nations which most damage the world's environment — the rich ones, that is — recognise that the harm they are doing is universal, affecting themselves as much as others. Consequently, they are taking some steps to limit it. But we may question how possible it is to do so adequately within the present framework of global society and its guiding attitudes.

I believe that these enormous issues can only be resolved by moving towards the type of world-wide democracy, resource sharing and free of national sovereignties, that I have tried to suggest. To the extent that this matures, peace, development and environmental health will grow interdependently.

PART III
Education

Chapter Twenty Eight
The Scope of Education

It would be perfectly reasonable to say that everything in these pages is about education. The philosophical (or should I say psychological? — there is a point where the two seem to merge) basis of everything I am trying to convey, is that unless we can manage to draw out, encourage and nourish our inner potentialities and those of others we shall achieve nothing of value. This is precisely what education means: to lead out. But much of the time we think and behave — in the class room, the lecture hall and indeed everywhere when we are informing our friends, children, colleagues and the rest about anything as though what we must do is to *shove in*. For most people shoving in information, expertise, ideas, opinions, theories, is what education is all about. Of course some of it is necessary. If people wish to become doctors, stone masons, physicists, or in fact anything; if they want to learn about any subject such as french or geography or how to sole shoes, there is some information they must be given. But unless this is given in an *educational* way they won't acquire the capacity to use it properly. This means they must be helped to understand their own natures as well as the nature of what they are being told. Only thus can they bring to bear the full range of our amazing human abilities on whatever practical or intellectual task may face them.

Issues of development are certainly highly educational. They pose fundamental problems about the nature and purpose of society, yet the practice and theory of development have been based on the most naive and limited idea of what human beings need. The model of the ideal society towards which we are supposed to be striving is one of western-style affluence, and the more affluent the better. We in the rich nations are told that because we are well-off we shall give more to charitable schemes to help the less fortunate. What nonsense! We are as well-off as we are because most of us don't give a damn for the poor, either in our own country or abroad. We are swept up in the materialistic illusion that external conditions, especially riches, create happiness. If this were so happiness could be measured on the scale of wealth, with millionaires at the top. We know perfectly well that this is not the case, yet continue to believe the illusion. Education in this context means, especially, becoming aware of the reality that will dissolve this delusion and help us towards an understanding of what development might mean.

As for mediators, their work involves a constant effort to develop their own inner resources to resist fear, prejudice and blindness in their approach to the protagonists they are dealing with. This, however, is inseparable from their attempts to educate these people about each other, to dissolve the illusion that they are separate (and usually superior!) creatures, and without openly so doing, to bring their attention to their real being.

Most of the 'lessons' of education in these fields, and indeed in learning and teaching how to live more fully, effectively and compassionately in general are not 'taught' in any formal way. The people who have had most *educational* impact on me have not been my teachers in school or university — I have got very little from these except a certain amount of information. Nearly all my education has come from the many wise, kind and good people I have been fortunate enough to meet.

Nevertheless, relationships within the formal structure are very important. For one thing, they constitute the setting within which genuine education can take place. Teachers who respect, love and value the great potential within their students teach them far more than the arithmetic, history, science, etc.; they also *teach them about themselves and the world*. They teach them that within each of us there is something worthy of trust and affection. This makes young people feel happy rather than guilty about themselves and at the same time makes them more confident of the worth of others. It is to be expected as a result that they will also do better in their physics, French, English, and so on.

I should also point out that the converse is not necessarily true. Some most unhappy children do brilliantly because they are desperately trying to reassure egos menaced by insensitive teachers and to placate those teachers, symbols of angry parents whose love they feel they have forfeited through their badness. On the whole, however, the poor teacher, that is the one who does not *educate,* does very much more harm than good. Instead of educating, s/he *teaches* the lesson that we are both wicked and stupid and that adults in a superior position are cruel and cannot be depended on for help or comfort: this is a rotten start to life. Into the bargain, they may well ruin our intellectual capacity, at least for their particular subject(s).

I personally suffered from a particularly bad teacher of arithmetic when I was nine or ten. He would cuff us or hit us hard with anything that came to hand if we made any mistakes. From having greatly enjoyed the simple sums my mother used to set me as a very little boy, I came to dread and hate the subject.

Thereafter, in every maths class I attended, my mind went blank. I just couldn't understand what it was all about; the meaning of algebra, which I found fascinating when it was explained to me as an adult, was a senseless mystery in which for no known reason absurd rules had to be followed if one was not to be punished. When at the age of sixteen (I think) I had to sit the then school certificate examination, I had been bottom of my form (we had such archaic grading systems then) every fortnight for years. I knew, and everyone made sneering remarks to this effect, that I couldn't possibly pass. Since passing in mathematics was at that time a condition of university entrance, I saw — and I must say with little regret — my 'education' soon coming to an end.

This foreboding was borne out by the first of the three examinations I had to take in the subject. As I looked at the exam paper my mind assumed its normal grey and despairing blankness. To pass we had to get, I think, an average of 60% on the three papers. On the first, according to the school's provisional marking, I got 34%. When I had to take the second paper, however, I had an attack of flu and a temperature of 103F. In a concession probably impossible today, I was allowed to do the paper in bed. Somewhat tipsy with the fever, I approached the exam with complete insouciance. I found it very easy and got 85%. Two days later came the final paper. My fever had dropped to 101F, but I was still relatively carefree; this time I got 70%. Thus I was able to beat the 60% cut-off point, to go to the university and in good time to become a professor! I suppose I owe all this to the benign virus that gave me the fever which enabled me to surmount the barrier of anxiety and sense of worthless stupidity that had held me back. Clearly, however, it had not prevented me from taking in the relevant mathematical knowledge and understanding. These were stored away somewhere in my brain cells as, according to psycho-analysis, are unhappy repressed memories and, in the computer on which I write, various files which have been mysteriously lost. It only needed some shock to the system, a fever, an analyst or a computer uncle, to bring them to the fore.

From the outset of my practice as a teacher (I would not presume to call myself at that time an educator) I was influenced by both my own deplorable schooling and my time with the Tavistock Institute of Human Relations. I believed that groups of people having different roles, such as teachers and children, or head teachers and their staffs, should have been able, or enabled, to communicate sufficiently to collaborate in what was of interest to them both. Children, for example, should have been able to discuss openly with their teacher what there was in his behaviour or approach that confused or worried them; head teachers and staff should likewise have been able to sort out anything that made their relationship, and consequently their work, less effective than it should have been. Yet there were often barriers erected by conventional views of their roles: it would not be 'proper' for members of the two groups to talk to each other in this way, or they were afraid of the consequences of so doing, or neither understood what was upsetting them and so could not make any effective approach to the other.

To the extent that there was an impasse of this sort, things went wrong. Relationships were somewhat stilted, needless misunderstandings arose, often accompanied by hostility and resentment, and the purpose of the relationship — in the case of education, more understanding and better learning — was harmed.

The answer, as I saw it, was in the broadest sense democracy. Communications had to be facilitated (a key phrase) by any device that would bring the various parties together in a manner that encouraged frank and friendly exchanges. A new 'culture' as it were, had to be established in which all parties could play their part better to their common advantage. The skills required to achieve this end were something like those of a therapist. S/he must be able to diagnose the nature and source of the psycho/social hang-ups giving rise to an objectively unsatisfactory situation, and to identify the subjective feelings of anxiety or anger associated with it; these, like the sources of neurosis, were seldom understood by those involved. For these reasons, the work was sometimes referred to as social psychiatry.

During the early years of my professional employment (after my assays at anthropology) and before I began to teach, most of my work had to do with such problems.

The first was concerned with former British prisoners of war who, on return home after the end of World War II, were miserably unable to resume proper family relationships, were ill at ease at work, with neighbours and old friends and were in general dislocated from their home society: 'unsettled' was the word applied to them. The traumas of, for most of them, five years imprisonment in distressing conditions, the separation during bombing of their own country when they never knew if their loved ones had survived, the sense of failure at being captured, the feeling that they could never share their experiences, constituted an insuperable barrier against a peaceful return to their former lives.

The people responsible for their rehabilitation in what were called Civil Resettlement Units were those who subsequently set up the Tavistock Institute. My personal job was as research officer to the organisation in which tens of thousands of former PoWs were resettled. The basic principle of the CRUs was to create a setting in which the ex PoWs could re-establish links with family, world of work and new post-war Britain without the trauma of complete separation from the one institution they *could* cope with — the army. So they remained in specially organised camps, but went on leave every weekend, did 'job rehearsals' with local firms, learned about the complexities of post-war regulations and rationing, got health problems sorted out; they attended group therapy and had as many visits to the psychiatrist as they felt they wanted. Above all there was no military discipline — they had had their belly-full of that in prison camp. My particular job was to evaluate the measure of success the CRUs achieved in their task. It proved to be considerable.

My next assignment was in a group of five villages in south west

England. These were known for their low standards of farming, their falling populations and lack of amenities, and their general recalcitrance in dealing with officials of the county council and the Ministry of Agriculture. In these relations with authority they displayed one ingenious piece of social juggling; they chose to elect as their representative someone whom they heartily disliked, thus disassociating themselves from anything affecting them that was done on the council. They even rejected the idea of a bus service and street lighting in one village. There were no village shops, no employment, no one who left the village for work ever came back, the proportion of unmarried men was very high and the proportion of women very low. A diagnostic feature for general village decline was, in fact, the sex ratio of the inhabitants.

The village people were not happy. But the more unhappy they were, the more they cut themselves off from effective contact with the outside world. They seldom travelled and a trip to London made by one man several years ago was still a subject of wonder and discussion. (This was in 1947, before package holidays!)

I became very friendly with some of the few young farmers who were still enterprising and socially aware. They were much concerned about the apparently degenerating condition of their part of the countryside and deeply resentful of what they considered to be the neglectful ignorance of the authorities. A recent example of this particularly infuriated them. It seemed that they were to be allocated a quota of new council houses — which of course was fine, but no more, they said, than their due. What annoyed them was that the official plan was to erect them in an area which everyone in the village thought to be quite unsuitable, for many reasons I now forget except that, among other things, it was in a frost pocket.

I asked if they had made their views known to the county planning office. 'What's the use?' they answered. 'He'd pay no attention to us; we'd just be wasting our breath'.

This official was an acquaintance of mine whom I thought to be friendly, intelligent and fair-minded. I told him the story and he agreed at once to visit the village, talk informally to my friends there and look into the whole matter.

The visit went off very well. Each side was astonished at the reasonableness of the other, and before too long the official plan was changed in accordance with the suggestions of the villagers.

I was particularly interested that during the ensuing few months, the general hostility towards and withdrawal from the outside world that had marked the collective attitudes of the villagers showed signs of changing. A number of people signed up for evening classes, occasional lecturers were asked to the village by the local Women's Institute and trips were organised to places of interest within and even beyond the county. These were of course small, but I think significant, indications of a shift of outlook. A minor incident, the meeting with the county planner and its successful outcome, had apparently gone some way towards helping people feel part of a wider community. By abandoning to some extent their suspicious and hostile illusion of separation, they had moved a step closer to reality.

The final example of this aspect of education concerns an industrial and agricultural estate also in a rural area. This was run by a board of most enlightened and generous trustees who hoped to be able to demonstrate how country life could be restored both economically and culturally.

Their approach to running the somewhat complex estate was both humane and democratic. They looked after their people very well, making sure that the amenities were excellent and giving the employees what they felt to be a sufficient say in the life of the community through an estate committee composed of residents and employees, with one of the trustees in the chair. However, in order to further their plans they felt it necessary to exercise fairly tight control over the general development policy, which might mean closing down or opening up particular enterprises at any time. They also felt it essential to control conditions which ensured that they were able to attract as employees people with the appropriate, often very high, qualifications. They insisted, for example, on the right to allocate housing themselves and not delegate the task to the estate committee. This body, they thought, might be moved more by domestic considerations than by what was needed for the economic health of the estate.

It soon became obvious that life on the estate was not as happy as the delightful setting and good amenities would lead one to expect. There was an undercurrent of uneasiness and of resentment against the trustees collectively. As individuals some of them were much liked and admired, a fact which added an element of confused conflict to the relationship between them and their employees. How could the latter complain about people who were so kind and friendly, and who tried so hard to make them happy? But it was possible to let off steam about a *group* which included members who did not live locally and were not known in the same way as the resident trustees.

The resentment was based on the arbitrary (as it seemed) fashion in which the trustees would close down activities if they were not working out as had been hoped, thus depriving people of work and — an equally important point — their homes on the estate. These trustee fads or whims as they were called, were a source of ridicule, resentment and fear which was poisoning the atmosphere. The related question of housing allocation was equally fraught. The trustees, it was said, might decide that a particular individual was needed for a new project and allocate her or him a house over the heads of people in greater personal need. An additional source of disquiet and discontent was that occasionally housing was allocated to friends or relatives of the trustees.

But on the estate committee, which purported to care for the morale and social amenities of the whole outfit, all was sweetness and light. Innocuous matters, such as children's parties, would be discussed over tea and biscuits, but never these issues by which almost everyone was affected and which made almost everyone anxious and insecure.

It seemed to me that the best way to approach this problem was through the estate committee which had, more or less, the right terms of reference although it was inhibited in its deliberations and decisions. It was necessary, in the first place, to persuade the rank and file members of the committee that it was 'safe' to raise these sensitive issues, and that to show some dissatisfaction was not just a demonstration of ingratitude and/or insensitivity to the needs of the estate; and to overcome the fear that if raising these issues gave offence, they would be punished arbitrarily and with no redress. As for the trustees and their advisers, it was essential to persuade them that if the committee were permitted to allocate housing (this soon became the key issue), they would not abuse their power.

I argued the trustee case to the ordinary committee members and was relieved to find that they accepted it at an intellectual level. This, however, didn't make them less anxious; they still thought, not unreasonably, that their lives were somewhat insecure. But I became convinced that this insecurity would be greatly alleviated if they were *trusted* to exercise a measure of judgement over these issues that meant so much to them. I believed that if this were to be done, their reduced anxiety would ensure that they made sensible decisions in the interests of the whole community and not be swayed by more personal concerns.

This case was put to the trustees who were basically sympathetic, but said that though I might be right, the ordinary members of the estate had not on the whole behaved responsibly. I answered that when people do not have responsibility, they cannot be expected to behave responsibly; they are more likely to be either apathetic or bloody minded.

The question was: how could the committee demonstrate its maturity before it had, in fact, had a chance to develop it by the exercise of responsibility. I spent several weeks talking with everyone concerned and afterwards a group of committee members drew up a proposal for a fresh constitution. This put forward proposals for taking over housing allocation and several other slightly less important changes, such as authority to deal directly with the county authorities on certain matters. These were so well done, showing such a grasp of both detail and the difficult issues involved, as well as a wise sense of balancing the needs of individual and community, that they were all accepted.

Certain inherent conflicts, of course, survived. For example, the trustees still owned the houses and would continue to do so. They were the employers and would both initiate and bring jobs to an end. But at least the difficult and painful problems which would inevitably arise were now open to straightforward discussion, or at least more so. Some improvement of morale seemed to follow.

The three cases discussed here seem to me to be both educational and developmental; developmental because they are to do with the removal of blockages to growth and the fulfillment of human and social purpose; educational because they are to do with drawing out capacities for understanding by removing barriers of anxiety and suspicion.

I was working on these cases in the late 1940s. It was some years before I got involved, in sequence over the next thirty and more years, with education in the sense of more formal teaching, Third World development, international mediation, and the Tibetan Buddhist philosophy which has shaped my understanding of all these fields.

Looking back today, I am rather surprised to realise that my approach of forty years ago, though fragmentary compared with that of more recent years, was not inconsistent with it. I felt that health — mental or physical — was wholeness. By this I meant interconnectedness through what I have since termed peaceful relationships; by contrast pain and sickness were at the same time the cause and the result of separation. I argued that inner disunion, conflict within the individual's psyche, led to separation from our fellows; our inner conflicts were projected onto them, and they were then seen as alien and hostile. I still think this way, and also see that, paradoxically, the more we are inwardly fragmented, the more we are concerned with ourselves. Thus we continue the cycle of separation, illness and aversion, rather than that of unity, health and compassion. What I did not realise at this stage, or indeed for many years, was that these 'realities' were not the ultimate reality. This I now recognise as the complete interdependence, and hence the lack of separate 'selfhood', of all beings, to which I referred in the Introduction. There are different realities. One is quite properly called 'conventional'; it conforms to more or less accepted patterns of life and human behaviour (though it is 'relative' in the sense that these are impermanent, changing from age to age and from culture to culture) and within its own context it is fairly consistent.

Conventional or relative reality in the case of the former prisoners of war I have been discussing would involve relationships which were 'normal' or 'well-adjusted' (in the sense of evoking no adverse comment) in the family, at work, or in the community. (It was interesting, however, that men who were respected as being 'good fellows' or 'doing very well' had relationships with wives and others which seemed to transcend the average somewhat humdrum stability: the hallmark of these relationships was flexibility and co-operativeness rather than rigid adherence to the norm.) Destructive deviations from the norm, such as domestic violence, attacks on neighbours, or refusal to work contravened the conventional social or psychological standards and were adjudged in varying degrees unreasonable or undesirable, or as criminal or sick. This may be thought of as a second degree of conventional reality.

In the case of the villages, the second degree of conventional reality could be defined in terms of the paranoid and self-defeating fears and suspicions of the county authorities and indeed of any 'foreigners', as all outsiders were termed (as opposed to 'foreigners from abroad'). These exaggerated anxieties in fact stood in the way of the villages moving towards the realm of regular conventional reality where tolerable working relations exist with such bodies as county councils, and whole categories of people are not lumped together as hostile. In the case of the estate, the conventional relationship was the effective collaboration between the trustees and their employees towards which I was working through the estate committee. As in the villages, the second degree of conventional reality was the anxious lack of trust which inhibited both sides in achieving this.

Generalising somewhat, we might say that in the first, the 'normal', level of conventional reality, we may experience feelings such as fear, dislike, anger and longing; these are justifiable and reasonable within the assumptions of convention, but they would fade before the brightness of ultimate reality. However, the emotions associated with the second degree are by every standard irrational. 'Reasonable' apprehension is transformed into absurd panic, irritation into fury, mild dislike into hatred, and so on. We may need to gain liberation from this 'neurotic' type of relative reality before we can cope with the far more taxing difficulties of liberation from the 'normal' type. (But we must beware of facile judgments. Women and men moving towards enlightenment may speak and act in a manner that seems bizarre or sick to the conventional; this has led to the persecution of many saints and seers by the 'healthy'. I was even aware that some of the former prisoners of war who were most positively resettled, and on that account were admired by their friends, could in fact forfeit approval by progressing too far beyond the accepted conventions. Here lie great dilemmas and difficulties for those who see through the limitations of the status quo. We should bear in mind the Hindu precept that life is an illusion, a game which we must understand as such, but play with skill and grace.)

This section has dealt with what are in the widest sense educational approaches to questions of social pathology. The next one is concerned more specifically with education in the more usual setting of school and university. It leads into deeper issues of that transformation of awareness by which we may eventually glimpse more clearly the ultimate behind the conventional, conditional, and relative reality.

Chapter Twenty Nine
Learning and Teaching

In a complete, or one might say, peaceful educational relationship, teachers do three things: they draw out the students' potential not just for learning but also for living, they impart actual knowledge and they themselves learn — any PhD who thinks s/he has nothing to learn from a five year old should go back to school!

Sadly, however, it is seldom really like this. One reason perhaps is that education — or it would be better to say schooling — has largely been captured by a society governed by the spirit of competitive materialism. To the extent that the character and content of education is increasingly dictated by the needs of the market, it is dominated by the acquisition of useful skills. I don't mean necessarily such things as computer programming or inorganic chemistry and the subjects that lead up to them, but also interpretations of history and social studies that emphasise a particular set of values and objectives desirable for success. By success, I mean the achievement of possessions, position, power and of course wealth that customarily are thought necessary for the reinforcement and gratification of the ego, of 'I'.

Thus education to a large extent has become the tool of a materialist and capitalist civilisation, and teachers, idealistic and good though I believe the majority to be, have at least outwardly to conform to its demands. They have to teach certain subjects and they must teach in such a way that their students pass examinations in them. When I was teaching in Africa, this greatly distressed some of my colleagues who tried to introduce variety and interest into the curriculum. The students were initially excited, until one asked 'Is this in the syllabus?'. When told it was not, they all demanded that the teachers should stick to the official and extremely humdrum text books.

A malign result of utilitarian education is that it has become very uninteresting. Only those who are 'good' students and see it as a means of satisfying aspirations stimulated by press or television and thus of satisfying 'I', work diligently. Those who are 'bad' students have little incentive to do so, and are in varying degrees bored, inattentive and rebellious. They leave school virtually uneducated in the double sense of having neither learned anything — 85% of black and Puerto Rican children leave school in New York functionally illiterate — nor having their own inner potentialities for creativity, wisdom or compassion evoked and cultivated, at least in the context of the school.

In Britain today we are witnessing a remarkable abuse of what education ideally might be. State schools, attended of course by the great majority of children, are being desperately squeezed of money. Almost universally the most able and dedicated teachers are finding increasing difficulty in teaching with diminishing resources coupled with discouragement from government quarters, and are leaving the profession in droves. At the same time there is growing emphasis on the virtues of private education.

If present trends continue we shall have the educational pattern which is most appropriate for a society deeply immersed in the illusion that happiness (which is equated with virtue) is to be found in externals. The best education will be for the best people; which is to say the people best able to pay most for it. And so on down the scale until the people who are unable to pay at all will have the worst education. But this is really nothing to worry our leaders, who seem to believe that the children of the poor and unsuccessful are more than likely to have inherited their parents' propensity for failure; costly schooling would simply be wasted on them. However, their training would enable them to carry out simple, necessary tasks for their betters, and would not give them exalted ideas about equality.

These possibilities are profoundly disturbing, especially since the changes demanded by real development need the wholehearted co-operation of education, formal and informal. However, the picture I have painted is a caricature of what military strategists call the worst case. Systems are never truly monolithic or uniform. There is always a crevice in the great rock where a flower can grow and which the frost will then widen until the stone cracks open.

I first became directly involved with pedagogy as head of a university department of education and psychology which was largely concerned with teacher education. I was very conscious of my own experience as a student at both school and university. During a dozen or so years at school I can only remember one teacher from whom I learned anything. It is true that over many years I absorbed enough french, latin, history and the like to scrape through the necessary examinations, but remember no intellectual excitement or even faint interest. I became particularly disillusioned with the whole business when, having been near the bottom of my class in english for several terms, largely because I couldn't master the system of parsing sentences, I won the school prize for writing poetry. Surely, I thought, this   means that I can use my language properly; why then all this nonsense about grammar? At the university I did, in fact, learn a great deal, but from living in a highly stimulating atmosphere, from my friends and from reading. It was, however, not until I shifted from history to anthropology after two years that I was fortunate enough to find two really great teachers, A.R. Radcliffe Brown and E.E. Evans Pritchard.

I attributed this, though not in so many words, to the fact that my teachers had had no help in developing a proper learning/teaching relationship. The ones at my school had had no guidance in making regular school subjects taught at a fairly low level at all interesting or significant. I simply learned enough to get me through the various tests and examinations — and then forgot, because boredom and oblivion are closely related. It may be that my school teachers were not very scholarly, but the same could not be said of my university tutors. Both lots were decent and sincere people, but they lacked the ability to stimulate or to establish rapport with students beyond the exchange of pleasantries.

One thing struck me at that stage, when my mind was still awash with anthropological topics: that they had never passed through *rites de passage* from the role of student to that of professional adult. One day they had been students, immature, incomplete, young people to be guided and helped, not capable of exercising responsibility; the next day, having acquired their qualification, they emerged like butterflies into a different world where their role was suddenly reversed.

One might say that teacher training constitutes a *rite de passage* and so it certainly should, but my school — being a private one —

had no trained teachers, and few university teachers have had any preparation for teaching beyond the study of their subject. But even the year of teacher training for which I was now responsible, despite its weeks of teaching practice, seemed to hold them back until they were through it. The whole approach to their instruction seemed no more than a continuation of the schooling which they, now in their early twenties (except for a number of veterans of military service) had experienced for the previous sixteen or seventeen years.

I resolved to try to develop the year's work into a process of transformation from the student role as learner to the teacher role as educator in as full a sense as was possible within the existing system. First of all it was necessary to revise the curriculum. In the short time available the students were expected to master snippets of topics so diverse as the history of education, the philosophy of education, physical education, sex education, the physical and emotional development of the child, school drama, educational psychology and testing, as well as teaching methods in their particular subjects — a doughy mass of unpalatable and indigestible material to be vomited out in a series of examinations at the end of the term. I soon learned that the students both detested and despised the examinations: they were irrelevant to the profession they were to join, they could be passed after a crash programme of cramming shortly before the examinations and then forgotten, and they were a humiliating because unnecessary prolongation of the student status.

It was necessary of course to do more than alter the curriculum; the manner of teaching was even more significant and more inappropriate than what was taught. These students did not need lectures. What they wanted was exploration and discovery. Most of the instructional time, therefore, was now spent in seminars built around the sorts of issues they would come across — or would already have in teaching practice — in the class room. These could then be related to psychological or other theory, rather than learning about the theory in abstract. Examinations also had to go. They were a worthless method of assessing whether or not these young women and men were suitable as teachers. They were evaluated, therefore, in terms of written or spoken contribution to seminars and on the basis of their effectiveness in the class room during the period of teaching practice. The pattern of learning/teaching which evolved was to a great extent worked out with the students themselves. Indeed, being trusted with the planning of their own education was an important part of the whole educative process, the movement from the passive (as it had been) world of the student to the active one of the teacher, who would no longer (as used to be said of school masters) be a man among boys and a boy among men.

Finally, the grading system was abolished. Previously the certificates awarded had been graded into classes, as are honours degrees. This, I discovered, offended the students. They felt they had spent a year working as colleagues with people who would in the future be colleagues in the teaching profession. For some to be singled out as somehow superior to others seemed invidious. Interestingly it was the more able students who were particularly insistent on this point.

All this happened over thirty years ago and there have been many educational changes since then. I have changed, too. I would still think that the sort of things I did were right, but I realise that the spirit in which I did them was highly elitist. I was trying to establish a democracy, because my recent experiences had shown me that democratic societies were more effective than authoritarian ones; but contradictorily I was trying to do so by diktat! Although I thought I was working through consultation and consensus, I was rather high-handedly imposing my ideas on a compliant staff.

Some ten years later, after very different interludes in Asia and Africa, I moved another step onwards (I trust) towards bringing my understanding and practice of education closer to conformity with the reality of our nature. I was at this time at Harvard where my classes consisted for the most part of very mature students, many from the Third World and from American minority groups — Blacks, Chicanos, Puerto Ricans, Native Americans, the remainder being white post-graduates. The classes were to do with issues of development and social change, and with the part of education in these processes.

I think that on the whole I was a good teacher. I liked my students very much and took a great deal of care over their work. But I also took a great deal of care to maintain what I considered to be high academic standards. These involved a degree of rigour in the presentation of work. It had to be sufficiently long to do justice to the subject. Ideas had to be substantiated by the right references and quotations (it now amazes me that any absurd statement can be justified quoting another idiot who has had the same ridiculous thought!). References, notes and bibliography had to be set out just so. And of course especially good marks would be awarded to those students who had had the good sense to write the sort of things I was known to like; I didn't think of them as sycophants or even as enterprising which was closer to the mark, but was vain and egotistical enough to consider that they showed scholarship.

But in the period of ferment and change, inner and outer, that I have described at the beginning of this book I began to see my part as a teacher, and my relationship with my students, quite differently. We were the same: we were one. I perhaps knew a few things which it would be good to pass on to them, but they also had things which I would profit from knowing. Unfortunately, academia fosters the view, alike in teachers and taught, that the knowledge, thoughts and experience of students are worthless; but I now saw that this was not so and that one of my tasks was to convince my students of this. I must convince them of their inherent wisdom, not to make them self-satisfied but proud of the shared human inheritance of divinity and eager to reveal it in its full panoply and power.

In practice what this meant was that I abandoned the standards I had set, the careful marking in which I would brood on the merits of a paper and whether it should be awarded A- or B+. I gave up the effort to *direct* the students in any particular way. At the beginning of the course of seminars I said something like this:

We are going to explore together the subject of mediation (or development or whatever was to be the main emphasis). None of us knows all about it but everyone knows something about it. Simply through having lived to our present ages we have experienced all the most crucial human situations. We have loved and feared and been happy and miserable; we have been lonely and we have rejoiced in the company of friends; we have felt the wonder of creation and the heaviness of boredom and depression; we have experienced peaceful and unpeaceful relations; have been angry and resentful and jealous; we have faced difficulties and pains and have both overcome and been defeated by them. You may ask why this is relevant to the study of mediation, but mediation is essentially a human problem and we meet its challenge equipped with our knowledge of these fundamental human conditions which, though universal, are experienced differently by all of us.

I will not presume to grade you on what you say or write. I only want you to feel free to express what you feel to be important in the best way you can. Don't worry about what others, particularly I, might think. Whatever you do you will certainly pass the course. Even if you say nothing you will pass. Even if you don't attend you will pass. I don't propose to give any grades at the end, but if any of you feel you would like one, I shall give you an A. (I knew that some of the Native Americans who had been financed by their tribes to attend felt that their sponsors would be delighted by concrete evidence of success. I was happy to provide this. The few who asked for grades and consequently were given As, did work which by any standards would have merited them.)

Some of my colleagues predicted that this approach would be disastrous; the course would be treated as a soft option to which people would flock in order to get by without doing any work. I predicted, rightly, that only the serious, who were more interested in real learning than marks, would attend. And so it turned out. The meetings of the seminar were a ferment of excitement; although no one was forced to produce written material most of them did and those who didn't planned debates or displays of high quality. I was greatly struck by the unusual quality of the work. Although it may have lacked the academic polish I had pedantically demanded in the past, it was imaginative and creative and dealt with real issues. I remember asking one young woman how it was that the quality of the contributions of the class was so high. 'That's easily explained', she said. 'In most of our seminars we are writing to please the teacher. In fact we study the professors more than the subject — that's what we did with you before. Now we are pleasing ourselves by studying what interests us in a way we feel to be appropriate'. She went on to explain something I had already expected: that many of the students did not believe what I had told them about the lack of requirements for passing. They thought at first that it was another crafty professorial trick, and were very wary until they had made sure that it was not.

My role as a *teacher* had several aspects. I began the series of seminars by setting a sort of intellectual framework; or, if that sounds too rigid, of explaining how I looked at the subject. This, I told the class, might be considered as a point of view, among many others, which might help them to get started — if only by disagreeing. Once the discussions of papers and presentations got going, I was on hand to suggest questions or interpretations if necessary — often it wasn't; a friend from a neighbouring university who had heard of my classes came as a visitor to one of them. 'It was very interesting' he said afterwards, 'but you didn't open your mouth'. And that was true. There was no need; the students had taken over, and I was just enjoying listening to a wonderfully interesting exchange. This introduces my third main role: as learner. When a group of people are genuinely exchanging experiences and insights, everyone who is open to it has much to discover: the 'teacher' becomes a partner in learning.

Paradoxical though it may sound, what I have just described has some of the quality of the guru-chela relationship. It is well known that students are supposed to revere their gurus and to obey them without question. But gurus also revere their pupils, seeing that they already have the wisdom which they, the gurus, have to awaken and make manifest — *not to impart*. What they do impart is the *method* but not the *wisdom* itself. The essence of the learning/teaching relationship is an exchange of wisdom. This can only occur when there is profound mutual respect. It is respect that is lacking in so-called education based on shoving in — opinions, prejudices, facts frequently distorted by the quirks of the teacher — instead of drawing out wisdom and other of the great universal qualities.

Finally I might comment that one delightful result of these seminars was that I became close friends with many splendid young people and that barriers of race, which I began then to appreciate had been high, were broken down. An objective proof of this is that I became the godfather of a black baby.

There can be little doubt that education, in both the general and the specific sense of what happens in schools and colleges, must be crucial in all attempts to halt or slow down the disastrous spread of the three poisons which are so sorely contaminating our world. But how can that be effected on a sufficiently large scale? The examples I have given out of my own experience are paltry, included only as examples of a sort of 'teaching' which many wiser and more experienced women and men have practised and written about. In my case, too, I was fortunate to be working in institutions where I was much less constrained by officialdom than are most teachers.

I hope, however, that something of the *spirit* underlying true education can be maintained even in the most adverse of institutional circumstances. Basically everything depends upon how we understand our own nature and that of those we are dealing with, whether they be students in school or university, our own children, protagonists in war, officials concerned with development, and so on. So long as we see 'I' as the central actor instead of as an illusion, the three poisons will go unchecked, we will in fact contribute to their lethal potency. But to the extent that we realise our emptiness of ego we shall be able, whatever our circumstances, to detoxify them.

Conclusion

My purpose in writing these pages has been twofold. In the first place, I hoped to demonstrate how the great illusions of 'I', of separate self-existence and the resultant three poisons, has spawned terrible outbreaks of violence, is turning our precious biosphere into a toxic desert, and giving rise to infinite sufferings by blinding us to the ultimate reality. Secondly, I wished to suggest how, to the extent that we are conscious of that reality, we might work against the poisons.

I chose as examples, the three types of activity in which I had been engaged throughout my adult life: peace making, mainly in the form of mediation, development, and education. The things that went wrong and those that went more or less right seemed to illustrate some of the chief issues.

Of course the three sorts of work were superficially very different. Peace making could be typified as trying to help the protagonists in a bloody struggle to find their way out of the trap of violence; development, as measures to improve the quality of life, especially in the Third World; education, as building a relationship between teacher and student which enabled both to grow.

In a more generalised sense, however, they all flow together. The specific of one may be the politics and strategy of the battle field; of another, futurology, the planning office and the economics of poverty; of a third, the class room or lecture hall. Essentially, however, they are all concerned with human beings, their enslavement to a false, relative reality which may also be a very sick one, and their liberation from it. To the extent that we are liberated, we are free from ignorance and the fearful pressures of craving and dislike. Thus we are also more free to make wise decisions, to act with compassion rather than with compulsion, and to establish peaceful relations with others, whether they be 'enemies', or students, or indeed anyone we encounter in everyday life.

To this measure, in addition, we perceive all these people differently. They cease to be threats to 'I', or objects to be manipulated to reassure us of goodness and strength, or to assuage our guilt; they are no longer people to envy, hate or fear. They are human beings to cherish (rather than lavishing concerns on ourselves), to help towards liberation (rather than to grasp at as we grasp our ego), to *recognise as ourselves.*

Here I find a wonderful paradox. The more we understand that human beings are not self-sufficient, self-existent, and separate creatures, the more we appreciate and value their individuality. What we thought of as their personality was indeed their *persona,* the mask that ego fabricates and which conceals the reality of our nature.

That real nature, which we all share since we grow in and from the same ground of being and are truly the same stuff, is also infinitely various. Each of us is a prism that refracts differently the all encompassing light of creation, of omnipresent consciousness. Here I am again reminded of Indra's net. In this endless heavenly net there is a bead representing a human life at every intersection; each bead reflects and is reflected by every other. Even so, on this earth, everything we do, say or think affects every other human being and perhaps other forms of sentient life; an awesome responsibility and equally splendid opportunity for those who can radiate love rather than discharge a fog of negative emotions.

This is a realm of reality of which I have long been in some degree aware. However, the experiences on which this book has been based have transformed what were more or less intellectual concepts into something approaching actual knowledge. These experiences have been highly practical, but for me they have provided the link between the conventional reality of the suffering world about us and the transcendental one of ultimate reality.

For these reasons, I cannot agree with those, some of them Buddhists, who argue that our task is to work solely for our own salvation, our enlightenment, because only the enlightened can truly contribute to the well-being of their fellow humans; and who affirm that only those who have attained this high state can serve others in any useful way.

I believe instead that the seeds of compassion and wisdom within each one of us demand something more. The anguish of a neglected child or a hungry animal, of a war-torn nation or an oppressed people, cannot be passed by. And if we act out of kindness which, as the Dalai Lama has often said, is the basis of his religion, our wisdom and compassion will perhaps increase, and some pain and sufferings be thereby relieved.

What more can we do; what more can we ask?

Appendices

Appendix 1
Who Am I?

Virtually all our worst troubles stem from our failure to recognise the potentialities of our nature, with the further consequence that we think ill of ourselves — or at any rate of our fellows. Not understanding the good things, we over-estimate what we then imagine to be the bad ones.

Everything centres around the concept of 'I'. It is not only a question of whether 'I' is good or bad, but also whether 'I' is clever or foolish, pleasant or nasty, kind or cruel, interesting or boring, generous or mean, progressive or reactionary, dependable or untrustworthy, and innumerable other antitheses; and of course the same applies to all those others we call 'you'. We judge our fellows and we judge ourselves as entities to be defined by the qualities we ascribe to them, often more reflecting our own state of mind than anything else; and these qualities are probably not ones they, and perhaps others, would ascribe to themselves.

Most of us think we have a fairly clear idea of what we are like, our character, our capabilities, our tastes, our good qualities and our less good ones, our attractive and our less attractive features, what we like and what we don't like, what we expect of our friends, the part we are capable of playing in our family and in life in general, and so on. Those who can't define themselves in this sort of way are said to have an identity problem, and are prone to anxiety and uncertainty. Those who feel that the less positive part of their 'identity' predominates, are depressed; those who see only the bright side are cocky and optimistic. We are all, however, in varying degrees and different ways deluded about ourselves.

The delusion is not exactly that we are more, or less, what we think we are, more, or less, charming or whatever it may be, but that the whole concept of 'I' is wrong. There is, of course, a human being,

Mary or Bill, who exists, but not as s/he thinks s/he does, as a separate, self-existent being, a *Ding an Sich*, associated with but essentially separate from all others. This is usually *how we feel ourselves to be,* even if reason tells us otherwise.

We are in fact not only not independent, we are *inter*dependent with what we would have thought of as separate from us. The thoughts, opinions, ideas and habits of mind which we would designate as my thoughts, my opinions, etc., all originated in sources outside ourselves — books, the media, our teachers, parents, and so on. Our bodies are composed of cells from our father and mother and a genetic inheritance going back countless millennia to our prehuman ancestry, and of particles and energies that are, literally, ageless. Our place and role in the community, something inseparable from our view — however deluded — of ourselves, is a product of the interplay of social, economic and other forces acting upon us. Likewise this role constitutes part of the forces playing upon others, as do all the physical and mental components of our being.

For these reasons, it is more accurate to think of ourselves, not as separate beings, but as elements in a system in which all other elements, from the great to the minute, are in constant interaction with each other.

A delusion related to the delusion of 'I' is that, if only we can properly arrange the circumstances of our lives, we shall be able to achieve a desirable permanence and stability; this we see as a prerequisite for secure happiness, the major goal for most of us. But this is impossible in a system of total interaction. Everything that happens anywhere affects everything else. There is, for example, nothing we can do to prevent an obscure combination of events from precipitating the economic depression that unexpectedly ruins us; nor can we avoid the epidemic that kills our loved ones, nor the accident by which we are crippled; nor, to look at things from another angle, the happy coincidence that introduces us to the man or woman we love and marry. But such are the apparently great events of our lives. The seemingly trivial happenings, the shifts of mood (which will, however, have a considerable effect on those close to us and thence on those close to *them*) are equally the product of the convergence of countless forces, inner and outer. We are both the victims and the perpetrators of these incessant destabilising exigencies, happy or unhappy.

To counteract this inescapably evident instability, we try to emphasise the permanence of 'I', by referring to the self, or perhaps the 'real' self, or perhaps the soul, or something similar. This implies that, although the identity may be a bit fuzzy around the edges, there is nevertheless a stable and inviolable core, the true 'I'. But if there is such a thing, where is it to be located, in what set of thoughts, feelings or impulses; how is it really to be defined? The more we look for the real 'I' which we constantly claim to exist, the less, if we are honest, can we identify it.

Serious search will also reveal the impermanence of those attributes we might well have claimed for 'I'. We will be amazed and perhaps distressed if the hidden observer in our mind can watch (a difficult exercise) our feelings flicker across the screen of consciousness. The train of association leaps, uncontrollably erratic, from one memory to another bringing an equally rapid shift of unrelated emotions — now a tinge of depression, now of excitement, of anxiety, pleasure, or guilt.

If we are particularly watchful we will notice something else. Our dominant 'I' varies considerably according to circumstances, the mood we are in — angry, infatuated, excited, intellectually stimulated, worried; and the company we are keeping — those we like, dislike, feel inferior to, or wish to impress in the different ways in which we hope to impress lovers, employers, colleagues, and so on. In each 'I' mood we will have different hopes and ambitions, different fears, likes and dislikes, even a whole different approach to life — dashing or cautious, materialistic, hedonistic, austere, out-going or withdrawn. Who are we? Which one is 'I'?

On the whole, however, we tend not to be very observant retrospectively, still less so at the time. Our general level of awareness is low. (I could use the word consciousness, or awakeness, but I employ awareness because its root implies also watchfulness, and hence attention and control which are the keys to the proper understanding, development and use of our potential.) Much of the time we are so unwatchful as to be in a sense asleep. We hurry from one room to another to do or fetch something, but when we get there we cannot remember what it was.

Our unwatchfulness is associated with the automatic character of much of our activity. Just as our thoughts dart unbidden from one recollection to another, following an infinitely complex path of neural connections, so we play out even the most elaborate patterns of behaviour without any thought; all that is needed is the stimulus of a particular signal. This could be the alarm clock bell that wakens us in the morning. Because the brain, like a wonderful computer, has stored the information needed to carry out all the subsequent operations, we get out of bed, wash, dress, eat breakfast, and set out for work *without the need for thought, that is for watchfulness: the machine, as it were, does it all.*

The automatic function is, obviously, essential. If we had to relearn the procedure for tying shoe laces, fastening buttons or driving a car everyday, life would be impossible. There are some things that have to be left to the machine, like the workings of the cardio-vascular system, the digestion or the endocrine glands (though some would say that really awakened women and men can control them). If we remain sufficiently aware when issues involving human relations or moral judgement are concerned things will not go too wrong, but if the machine takes over on matters like these, with which it is unqualified to deal, disaster is almost inevitable. This is because our automatic function has usually come to incorporate not only such useful 'muscle memories' but also irrational responses based on old hurts, fears, angers and the like. These may be evoked in some sorely inappropriate manner by random trains of association. It is as though the driver of an automobile has been ousted by the machine, which then careers mindlessly down the highway until it crashes.

The word mindless is appropriate here. Automatism is mindless as is, indeed, the 'I', the false identity. It is an automatic learned response to either threat or the possibility of gain. When we say of some foolish or unworthy action, 'I must have been out of my mind', or of some stupid forgetfulness, 'I was absent minded', we speak no less than the truth. The actor was indeed very far from his or her real mind.

If, then, the 'I' is both illusory and indescribable, what kind of purpose does it serve?

It would appear to arise to help us cope with guilt, loneliness and fear resulting from separation from a more genuine part of our nature. We sense dimly or sporadically the existence of this part, but cannot grasp it, and so try to make do with the fraudulent and deceptive identity which we fabricate automatically and unconsciously with the machine-like capacities of our mind. We build it up out of scraps of information providing some sort of evidence of an acceptable 'I'. It is tailored in the first place to satisfy ego and then, with luck, other people. Into its composition goes everything that seems to give us reality and attraction — we take our pick of achievements, physical attributes, sensitivity of taste, courage and other moral qualities, a solid and reputable background, the fact that we are (apparently) loved by children, spouse, or at least faithful dog. We choose, part consciously, part automatically, what qualities and characteristics to stress in presenting ourselves to ourselves and to others. The resultant 'I' or series of 'I's, is an enormous edifice, parts constantly being added, or altered or removed. We have been working on it since babyhood, this illusion in which we are wrapped.

Each one of us, as we have discussed, has a number of 'I's, just as we may have different outfits of clothing for different occasions. But each of them is not only transient — for the constantly changing system of which we are part will call for different self-presentation — but in jeopardy. The things on which we depend for a gratifying sense of self are fragile: if athletic prowess, we may lose a match and in any case grow old and less able to compete well; if physical beauty, we also grow old and may in addition suffer disfigurement or become obese; if intellectual achievement, our views may be derided as out-dated or silly and our book panned by the critics; if our handsome and athletic son, loved as a credit to his father's 'I', turns out a drug-addicted layabout reflecting discredit; if our apparently devoted spouse runs off with someone else — in all these and countless other emergencies the things that gave us a pleasing self-image now give us comparable anguish. To cap them all, perhaps we are bitten by the faithful dog! It is not just that hurtful things have happened and that we are unhappy, but that our sense of ourself as a worthwhile human being has been shattered.

We desperately try to repair the damage — we lost the match because we were out of form or the umpire unfair; the critic was biased; the son was really a fine lad misled by bad friends; and so on. We rebuild the self-image as best we can; if we can't, we fall into what is called a depression.

Generally, however, this false view of our identity drives us into two areas of feeling that deeply affect all our activities. The first of these can be characterised as craving: we want, long for, desire, lust after, are greatly attached to — possessions, money, power, particular people, experiences, states of mind, qualities, ideas, and so on and so on. I would emphasise that these aspects of craving do not merely consist of enjoying or wanting to enjoy whatever it might be, but the feeling that our whole being depends on it for *reality and identity*.

The other area of feeling can be characterised as hating: we hate, dislike, envy, are jealous of, distrust, fear, suspect people and circumstances that might frustrate the gratification of or deride our cravings. This is not necessarily nor even often an extreme loathing. It is usually manifested as vague distaste for people and things that we feel to be somehow alien: oh, I don't think I much like so and so or such and such, we may say. But such 'harmless' aversions can escalate into rage and hostility if so and so or such and such impinge on us in a way we feel to be threatening.

Thus it is that many of the things that mar human existence — violence, greed, jealousy, prejudice, ruthless competitiveness and acquisitiveness — originate in the illusion of an 'I' which we build up to compensate for our inability to grasp the deeper reality of our being. Unable to give proper expression to the half-sensed intimations of another dimension of our existence, we have moods of guilt, loneliness and *unreality*. Guilt because we dimly feel things should be different. Loneliness, because the essence of our illusory 'I' is its separateness. Unreality, because this 'I' with which we identify our being *is* unreal. And just because it is so difficult to accept the unreality of our sense of self, we erect this monstrous structure to glorify it, to give spurious substance to what is completely insubstantial.

Does the absence of a real 'I' mean that Bill and Mary do not exist? Obviously not. These are bodies, aggregations of faculties mental and physical that have a recognisable existence and reality, but not the separate, self-existent reality in which we tend to believe. It is a relative or conditional reality in the sense that it exists, shiftingly, only in its relationship to all other such realities.

This may not be a very reassuring definition of what we all feel to be something more solid, permanent and distinctive, but we can go

beyond this somewhat cold comfort. We all know that the 'I' as I
have described it is not the only expression of our being. We are not
entirely motivated by the cravings and hates generated by being
ignorant and/or out of touch with the foundations of our nature; life
would be intolerable if it were not softened and sweetened by
unselfish kindness, generosity and love. Remembering this, and
recognising that our unpleasant attributes are the fruits of illusion,
but not of *us*, will help allay self-hatred and guilt.

So what are we; what is our nature?

The aggregation of faculties — bodily functions and structure,
perceptions, emotions and impulses, feelings, and acts of
consciousness, what Hindus and Buddhists call the five *skandhas*, —
constitute the context of awareness. This is the consciousness that we
are empty of self in the false, mundane sense, while at the same time
we are elements in the universal system of interacting
interdependence.

The more vivid our awareness of this, the more we are liberated
from the toils of 'I' with its compulsive cravings and paranoid
hatreds. The more we are made free of our limited selves, the more
we are enabled to serve others who are entangled with the sufferings,
the fear, loneliness and self-loathing of ego. The more we recognise
our basic unity with others, the truth that we share, the same ground
of being, the more we feel for them as ourselves. The Christian
admonition that we should love others as ourselves can be
understood, some scholars maintain, to mean because they are the
same as ourselves. But be that as it may, the growth of awareness is
inseparable from the growth of compassion for the pain of others,
while compassion for their anguish also serves as a spur to develop
the awareness that enables us better to serve them.

Another doubt may arise. If we, together with all other
phenomena, are impermanent manifestations of this great universal
system — the void as some call it — must individuality also be a
myth? When we refer to a friend's good qualities are we deluding
ourselves, mistaking what is merely an expression of the ego for
something intrinsic to the person? Not necessarily so. Each aggregate
of the functions that comprise Bill and Mary, you and me, has a
different inheritance, genetic, social, and if you like, karmic. This
constitutes a sort of prism refracting differently in every case the

limitless and unquenchable light of what is universal and eternal, a miracle of diversity within unity.

We all refract this light as well as acting out the sorry dramas of 'I'. Hence the gentle, considerate and charitable aspect of our lives and behaviour, the altruistic goodness that transcends our greedy and suspicious self-seeking. The more we are aware of the essential goodness of our natures, the more readily will we realise our potential for enlightenment and fulfil our compassionate human purpose of helping others on the same paths.

And here is the answer to the question that headed this section: it is this everlasting essence, non-personal and ego-free yet unique and distinctive, that is the true nature of our being, the ultimate reality of our lives.

Appendix 2
Three Poisons

To the extent that we are ignorant of or insensitive to our own nature, we lose contact with the reality of phenomena. Because we are out of touch, so feeling a certain loss or inadequacy, we are driven to fabricate another reality, the 'I' which is also the eye through which we view the world. We see it as a dualistic world of 'I's and 'you's, goods and bads, friends and enemies, spirit and matter, this and that. Having no sense of a non-dualistic world of interconnectedness we create one around ourselves based on these dualities; what confirms 'truth' is good, what denies it is bad.

We long for these desirable things. They may be states of mind, types of relationship (dominant or perhaps submissive), qualities of character appearance or ability, power, possessions, position, any great or little thing, however simple or grotesque that somehow distinguishes us from and preferably sets us above our fellows. I know one man whose unfortunate life permitted him only to boast that when he had been in prison, it wasn't any ordinary old clink but a maximum security gaol where his mates had been the Great Train Robbers, as one might say that one had been at Harvard where one was a friend of John F. Kennedy.

All these attributes, qualities or achievements, real or imagined, are moulded together unconsciously into an identity, contradictory, complex, subtle and all-pervading. Although kaleidoscopically responding to every change, inner and outer, they give us the sense of self that shields us from the panic and disaster of not knowing who we are — but fearing the worst.

Many of the components of these 'I's, these false identities, are essentially crude. Even those woven around, for example, delicate questions of taste and artistic sensibility, can be reduced to such material things as books, paintings or hi-fi equipment. What matters is not just the ability to purchase such things, but in the process to purchase the envy of others. It is by such means that we feed the ego. We satisfy the craving for a sense of selfhood to fill the hollow hunger of ignorance by nourishment of a sort that confirms our existence and our goodness — as judged by the standards created by ourselves and probably our society. The more we get, the better; if it is moral qualities we crave, we may even ascribe to ourselves more humility or more modesty than X or Y!

In general, however, we need more of some quite straightforward commodity — a new car or a better hi-fi system. These satisfactions tend to be addictive and are required in increasing doses. I noticed this at the outset of my career. My 'I' was vastly gratified and enhanced the first time I was asked to give a public lecture. The second time, however, my delight was much less intense, my ego much less inflated. Does this mean, I asked myself, that I shall have to give increasingly prestigious addresses to get the same quota of self-satisfaction; and what happens to my ego if I don't?

All the time we are working to satisfy our craving, we are aware at the back — and occasionally at the front — of our minds that our happiness is transitory and precarious. We try to pretend that we only need x, y or z, perhaps a certain income level, a particular object, a particular person as friend, lover or possession to be happy for ever. But we also know that we may lose these things in a hundred ways. We may in addition be conscious that the whole argument is essentially unsound. If I may again quote from my own experience, I learned this at the age of five.

I yearned for a particular toy gun and pestered my mother to get it for me. At first, being a woman of peace, she refused. However she eventually gave in. I recall thinking to myself that I now had everything I could ever want and would be happy until the end of my life. But a day or two later I found myself weeping bitterly at some small disaster. No, I said to myself, lasting happiness can only come from an inner state and not from external things (not of course that I used those words).

Because happiness and identity, two conditions that overlap and intermingle, are in constant jeopardy, we are constantly alert like animals both in fear of predators and eager for our own prey, for what may harm and what enhance our fragile sense of 'I'. We dislike and/or fear people and circumstances that may diminish it. We envy those who have more of what we feel to be the happiness prescription (a pleasanter job, a finer house, more successful children). We are jealous of those who are doing better. We feel in varying degrees hostile to those who are different from us; because we don't understand them, we worry about what they might do to harm us. This accounts for much of the tension between the races, religions, classes, linguistic groups and perhaps the sexes.

In Tibetan iconography the relationship between ignorance, hatred and craving, what they term the three poisons, is symbolised by a snake, a swine and a cockerel. They circle endlessly gnawing at each other's extremities.

The basic human condition of enslavement to these inter-connected, mutually reinforcing negative feelings has led to certain recognisable patterns of thought and behaviour.

They have given rise to an active philosophy that is predominant in the westernised world. I would refer to it as competitive materialism. Competitive, because its objective is gratification gained by doing better than who or whatever may be the rival. Material, because in the last resort it can be reduced to the creation of wealth or power. This philosophy legitimises, almost sanctifies, what in other times and places might have been excoriated as greed.

No doubt the accumulation of property has for millennia, at least since tribes of herders and gatherers became settled agriculturists, a characteristic of human society. But the extremes of competitive materialism which confer high moral status on success are relatively new. Even in my life time I have seen them spread into remote corners of the world where, although some men were undoubtedly aggressive and self-seeking, this was not considered a virtue. As a young man, wandering in remote regions of the Middle East, the Balkans and Lapland, I learned that the most respected members of most communities were by no means the richest. They were admired instead because they were highly devout, or hospitable, or deeply versed in tribal tradition, or were poets or story tellers. The landlord or merchant may have been envied, but not admired.

Now, however, the values have changed. People are admired because they have been to the town, set up a business. Now their worth can be measured by the fact that they have a Mercedes Benz, or an air conditioned house, or even perhaps just a bicycle. Competitive materialism has spread like a moral plague.

The ignorance that impels us to seek a stable and satisfying sense of self through material means (craving) has obvious negative implications (hatred) for human relations.

In the most basic sense, to the extent that the 'I' is in control, we use people as things to serve our identity purposes. We may, of course, genuinely love them, but even so sometimes an element of ego may assert itself, rendering us at least temporarily insensitive or manipulative for our own inner ends; we try to evoke from them, irrespective of their own feelings and needs, the response that will gratify our 'I' or soothe its hurt . We can, in fact, be quite ruthless in the promotion and protection of 'I', manoeuvring those about us, including and perhaps especially our 'nearest and dearest'. To the degree that they submit and play our game, we reward them with love (that is to say, our favour); to the degree that they do not, they incur our enmity. Thus a man who claims to love his sons may compete viciously with them, attempting to assert his superior manhood (at least in his own eyes).

In this sense people become commodities, to be used like money or possessions, as building blocks for 'I'. But impermanence predominates. People and circumstances change in the constant flux pervading the system of which all are part; the woman or man to whom we look for gratification may withhold it, or perhaps our needs change so that s/he can no longer provide it. So a shadow of anxiety lurks below the surface of our mind, loaded with the potential menace of anger, hatred, resentment, jealousy or terror.

It is only to be expected that in situations where ego needs are institutionalised, such negative emotions form part of the pattern. Competitive rivalries and bitterness, ruthlessness towards the opposition or inadequate colleagues, though perhaps somewhat regulated by wise legislation, are accepted as part of the scene. If we manipulate our friends, we can certainly do the same to our competitors.

Thus the three poisons introduce their venom of anarchic heartlessness into all areas of our lives. Moreover, it spreads beyond the relatively humdrum doings of you and me and our personal and working relationships. It pervades our whole civilisation.

The psychological forces we have been discussing have crystallised into structures that dominate our lives. The vast network of economic institutions, from tiny business enterprises to the enormous transnational corporations, the banks and the stock exchanges, together provide a framework for almost everything we do. We may not like them, we may deeply disapprove of them, but for most of us it is almost impossible to do without them. Here let me pause to make an important point. I am not arguing that we should (if we could) abolish all such institutions; we do need some bodies to organise the production and distribution of goods of all sorts in our ever more densely populated planet. I am simply saying that although their functioning represents a genuine effort to meet essential human needs, it also reflects something else: this is the desperate rapacity that represents one aspect of our universal endeavour to gratify egos that are hurt, lonely and frightened because they are illusions, and are severed from the reality of being.

Nor are economic institutions the only ones utilised, created or perhaps hi-jacked by the collective 'I' of humanity trying to compensate for its plight. Almost any organisation can provide us with a chance to establish and confirm our sense of self; the club we proudly belong to, the learned society that confers status in our profession, the old school society that reminds us of the one time when we were important. All these and countless others provide the opportunity for us to succeed (and, of course, to fail); among them the political party provides perhaps the greatest scope. One type of institution is, however, perhaps most closely related to our main theme.

This is military, the armed services, the associated civilian organisations, the ministries of defence, the staff colleges, the arms factories, the intelligence agencies and so on. These serve (in our terms) a number of purposes. They offer the opportunity for domination and the expression of the violence often aroused by frustration and despair, they protect what our acquisitiveness has enabled us to collect, and they help us to gain control of, or to acquire, fresh sources of wealth.

The cancerous growth of these institutions, financial, political and military, has brought us to the brink of the abyss. They have become so swollen and monstrous that it is hard for us to connect them with something so personal as the demands of the false identity, the 'I'. But together they provide both the justification for and the means of our search for power position and thereby, and most importantly, of identifying ourselves. We take a deep pride in our group (whatever group is involved); our army is composed of 'our boys'; our money is, in a sense 'me'. All these are relations between a bogus 'I' and objects which are treated solely by the criterion of their service or disservice to our identity. This perhaps introduces a new idea that large groups of people may have a collective 'I' in the sense that circumstances can bring about a general concept of human and social needs and of how to gratify them.

I do not necessarily mean this in any quasi-mystical sense of a layer of consciousness shared by members of the same community or nation. We do, however, often seem to incorporate into our sense of self the fact of belonging to this or that nation, church, profession, organisation, etc. Our personal sense of self is then affected by what happens to the larger group. I have noticed this effect especially in the case of leaders of embattled nations: the valour of the troops is *their* valour, the victory *their* personal victory, the defeat *their* personal defeat. In this sense the opponent is not an impersonal enemy, but a personal one; he not only poses a material threat but a more subtle one to the 'I'. We hate him.

It would be an exaggeration to say that all institutions implicated with military or financial issues are direct crystallisations of the three poisons. Indeed this could not be said of barter economies, subsistence farming, police who in times of trouble protect their communities, or co-operative enterprises of many sorts. Nevertheless, the extent of activities attributable in the first place to acquisitive greed or to hatred is enormous and all pervading. For example, it has been calculated that at least 100 million people are engaged in work directly or indirectly involved with the military, mainly in Europe and North America, and that in the latter some 15% of the US work force is so engaged.

As I have said, such activities have no doubt always existed. However their present lethal interrelationship probably began to take shape around the end of the Middle Ages. Then a number of trends that have become closely interwoven began to develop. These were:
— The emergence of the modern state in embryonic form with the beginnings of a centralised administration, replacing such ramshackle agglomerations as the Holy Roman Empire.

— The development of armed forces to replace the somewhat haphazard assemblies of the armed retainers of nobles (who tended to drift away at harvest time!) for the temporary use of kings wanting to go to war.

—The birth of modern financial institutions, such as the Fugger bank, the Banco Giro of Venice, and the Exchange Bank of Amsterdam.

—A new philosophy, even theology, of wealth deriving largely from interpretations of the teachings of Calvin (but spreading to other branches of the Church and even to the Muslim world). These seemed to suggest that God showed his favour to those elected to join him in in the next world by showering on them material benefits in this one. Thus the idea that wealth and virtue were somehow correlated began to take shape.

—Science and hence technology, after a long period of stagnation, began to take off with the work of such as Galileo and Copernicus.

These five trends interacted in a variety of ways. The armies served the nations in their efforts to conquer and expand and so to acquire new national wealth to build better armies and thus to increase their resources. The banks and other financial institutions helped them in this respect. And as the business systems grew, so the political structures and principles within which they operated became better structured to the important goal of acquiring riches. The new philosophy contributed by promoting the spirit of capitalism. The emergent technology served not only by improving weaponry, but by facilitating the development of new industries and improving old ones.

This concatenation of conditions has contributed immeasurably to the state of the world as it is today: the high complexity of the global economy; the terrible sophistication of our weapons; the power that even the democratic state can exercise over its people; the ever growing gap between the rapacious rich and the poor; the forward surge of science and technology; the danger of universal destruction by nuclear war or accident, or the murder of the biosphere, dangers to which both of the foregoing have led.

To this sorry pass we have been impelled by the mindless and relentless pressure of the three poisons.

The arguments of the last few pages can be drawn together in a diagram showing the operation of the three poisons.

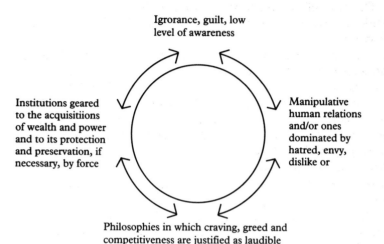

Igrorance, guilt, low level of awareness

Institutions geared to the acquisitiions of wealth and power and to its protection and preservation, if necessary, by force

Manipulative human relations and/or ones dominated by hatred, envy, dislike or

Philosophies in which craving, greed and competitiveness are justified as laudible motives

Lest this pessimism seem extreme, I would briefly mention here that the essential nature of humankind is also revealed in the many compassionate and creative developments which have occurred during the same period: a new and powerful if not yet sufficiently widespread spirit of universalism, countless agencies, small and large, public and private, designed to serve humanity both locally and internationally; a true sense of the interdependence of all things. A comparable diagram could be drawn to show how knowledge and compassion establish warm, unselfish and co-operative human relationships, generate the spirit of respect and reciprocal service and create institutions designed for the benefit of all. All this is indeed being done, but it could also all be lost.

There is currently considerable debate over the respective social roles of politicians and church people. The former tend to maintain that the latter should confine themselves to purely spiritual matters and leave questions regarding society and social policy to them. Church people on the whole reply that policies which adversely affect human well-being are not simply social but also have moral implications and hence a spiritual dimension.

I don't find it helpful to argue about dichotomies. That between spiritual and social seems to me to be false. Indeed I distrust the dualistic implications of the concept 'spiritual' which divides the world between what is pure and what is gross. I find it more helpful to think that we are all, in our separate spheres, engaged in the quest for reality. And reality is neither spiritual nor material, the concern of either politicians or clergy; it is as it is.

The preceding pages and the diagram try to show in a crude fashion how things affect each other. How one attitude of mind, ignorance, produces others, craving and hatred; how these influence our relations with others and the institutions we create; and how these latter affect our mental outlook, for we cannot be brought up in the ambience of institutions without being influenced by them. So, if we are concerned about one aspect of life, we must logically be affected also by all the others.

Appendix 3
Note on Aggression and Violence

It is often maintained that we are innately aggressive and violent, and that therefore attempts to establish conditions of lasting peace are bound to fail. But this proposition raises semantic issues which have to be considered first. In English usage the word aggression is generally taken to imply violence, while violence is taken to mean excessive and/or unlawful use of destructive force. In American usage, however, aggression is a prized quality; it is more or less synonymous with energetic, innovative, and vigorous pursuit of approved goals.

If we are all inherently aggressive in the English sense, the outlook for peace is admittedly bad. But what about the American sense? Let's first consider animals, whose behaviour is sometimes used to explain ours. Animals are certainly aggressive in the American sense in the pursuit of natural and unexceptional goals. They will fight among themselves to win or keep a mate, gain dominance in the herd or pack, safeguard the territory necessary to maintain their group or family, and to obtain food. However, they seldom kill their opponents; if so, usually by accident, and once their objective is gained, the aggressive behaviour comes to an end; they do not exert more force than is needed to safeguard their interests. Like the 'aggressive' American, their behaviour is more conducive to promoting peace and stability than the anarchic destructiveness that has stained so much of human history.

If, however, the inheritance from our prehuman ancestry has programmed us to be aggressive in the 'animal' or 'American' sense, how is it that we are in fact so wantonly, cruelly, and above all so pointlessly destructive? The Tibetan theory of the Three Poisons provides, I think, a very satisfactory explanation. Caught up in a world of illusion, desperately seeking gratification, we are full of irrational hatred for those who thwart us. We then fabricate every possible reason for our grotesque behaviour, calling on the most sophisticated distortions of religious, political or economic ideology to excuse the inexcusable.

However, some may need in addition, or instead, a more 'rational' explanation. It may be that we often have needs that cannot be gratified, either because of adverse conditions, such as extreme poverty or governmental oppression, or because they have been extended by artificially stimulated and unrealistic ambition. In such cases our frustration rises to a point where in desperation we fall upon each other or upon those we deem responsible for our plight; and again, of course, we employ every intellectual trick to justify our behaviour. It is worth noting that one of the few situations in which animals behave, as do humans, with extremities of violence against each other, is when rats, confined in extremely overcrowded cages and presumably suffering frustration of all their normal drives, fight and kill each other for no identifiable reason.

So no, we are not inherently and ineradicably aggressive and violent in the worst sense. But yes, the workings of the Three Poisons tend to evoke this behaviour to a greater or lesser extent in all of us. Fortunately, we are not entirely helpless. The wise teachers of humanity have shown us ways out of the wilderness of violence.

Since writing the above, I have come across the Seville Statement (see the Bibliography) which gives a brief but comprehensive summary of arguments for believing that human beings are not innately destructive.

Bibliography

I have divided the bibliography into sections that correspond to the three Parts and the Appendix. Although, as I have suggested, these merge and overlap at many points, it may make things clearer to maintain this somewhat artificial separation. The lists are short, not because the literature is scanty (though this is so in the case of mediation) but because much of it is irrelevant to my purpose. I don't intend to present a comprehensive overview of the subjects, but a few key works that may be interesting or helpful to someone wishing to amplify or pursue further what I have written.

Part I. Peace Making/Mediation

Bailey, Sydney, 'Non-official mediation in disputes: reflections on the Quaker experience' *International Affairs* 1985

Burton, John W., *Conflict and Communication*, London, MacMillan, 1969. *World Society*, University Press of America, Maryland, 1987.

Curle, Adam, *True Justice*, London, Quaker Home Service, 1981. *In The Middle*: Non-Official Mediation In Violent Situations, Berg, Leamington Spa, 1986.

Fisher, Roger, and William Ury, *Getting to Yes*, London, Hutchinson, 1983.

Galtung, Johan, *Essays in Peace Research*, Vol.II, PRIO Monographs,Copenhagen, Christian Eilers, 1976. ibid. Vol. III. 1978.

Yarrow, C.H. Mike, *Quaker Experiences In International Conciliation* New Haven, N.J., Yale University Press, 1978.

Part II. Development

For the most part, the works referred to below are highly critical of, or even antipathetic to, a great deal that is carried out in the name of development. It is sadly true that the pessimistic analyses of works published in the 1960s and 1970s is shown as being only too correct in those appearing in the 1980s. On the whole we have paid little attention to the wretched experiences of the poor.

The titles referred to here should perhaps be supplemented by reports of institutions which have made a genuine contribution to the relief of poverty in the EDCs. These include such private agencies as Oxfam, and such international ones as the United Nations Children's Fund (UNICEF) and the International Fund For Agricultural Development (IFAD). It is perhaps significant that neither agency gets anything like adequate funding from governmental sources. I would also recommend anyone interested in current development issues to subscribe to *The New Internationalist.*

I do not know of any body of literature, apart from what has come out of Tanzania and possibly bodies such as the World Federalists on which I am not well-informed, that promotes the type of democracy I have advocated. My list is therefore, somewhat limited

The Arusha Declaration, and TANU'S Policy on Socialism and Self-Reliance, Dar es Salaam, The Publicity Section, Tanu, 1967.

Bennet, Jon, with Susan George, *The Hunger Machine,* Cambridge, Polity Press, 1987.

Dumont, Rene, *False Start In Africa,* London, Sphere Books, 1966.

Curle, Adam, *Education for Liberation,* London, Tavistock Publications, 1973.

Frank, Andre Gunder, *Capitalism and Underdevelopment in Latin America: Historical Studies of Chile and Brazil,* New York Monthly Review Press, 1967.

Friere, Paulo, *Pedagogy of the Oppressed,* New York, Herder and Herder, 1970

George, Susan, *How the Other Half Dies:* The Real Reasons for World Hunger, Harmondsworth, Penguin Books, 1976.

Nyerere, Julius K., *Ujamaa: Essays on Socialism,* Dar es Salaam, Oxford University Press, 1968.

Sen, Gita and Caran Grown, *Development, Crises and Alternative Visions: Third World Women's Perspectives,* London, Earthscan Publications Ltd, 1988.

Worsley, Peter, *The Third World,* London, Weidenfeld and Nicholson, 1969.

Part III: Education

There is certainly no shortage of literature on education. However, except in the field of primary schooling where the insights of psychology have been admirably blended with innovative practice and humane concern for children, there have been very few basic changes in educational theory and practice during the last half century. There have, of course, been many wise and sensitive teachers, (John Holt is such a one), who have enriched educational literature with their insights. But basically I really only hear variations on ancient themes. I would, however, except the educational work of Rudolph Steiner, who seems to me to have related the methods of teaching to the spiritual realities of our existence. This fascinates me, since this is what I have tried to do in a very modest fashion, in the work described in this book. But apart from him, I can only think of that bizarre and inimitable genius, A.S.Neale of Summerhill. This list, therefore, is even shorter than the others:

Curle, Adam, *Education for Liberation*, (see list for Part II).

Friere, Paulo, *Pedagogy of the Oppressed* (see list for Part II).
Holt, John, *How Children Fail*, New York, Pitman Publishing Corporation, 1964.
Neale A.S., *Summerhill, A Radical Approach to Education*, Gollancz, 1962
Harwood, A.C., *The Recovery of Man in Childhood*, Anthroposophic Press, 1982 (Rudolph Steiner education)

Appendices

I mention first a selection of works on Tibetan Buddhism that I have found particularly helpful, and secondly a more varied collection of books that have enlightened me on the realities of our nature; these include those by McAllister and Capra that I have already mentioned, and one by John Blacking whose help I acknowledge in the Foreword.

Blofeld, John, *The Tantric Mysticism of Tibet:* A Practical Guide, London, George Allen and Unwin, 1972.

David-Neel, Alexandra, *Magic and Mysticism in Tibet*, London, Souvenir Press, 1967.

Angarika Govinda, Lama, *Creative Meditation and Multidimensional Consciousness*, London, Mandala Books, 1976.

Gyalwa Gendun Drub, His Holiness the First Dalai Lama, *Bridging the Sutras and Tantras*, compiled and trans. by Glen Mullin, Dharamsala, India, 1981.

Tenzin Gyatso, His Holiness the Fourteenth Dalai Lama, *Kindness, Clarity and Insight*, Ithaca, New York, Snow Lion Books, 1984.

Harvey, Andrew, *A Journey to Ladakh*, London, Jonathan Cape, 1983.

Kelsang Gyatso, Geshe, *Clear Light of Bliss*, London, Wisdom Publications, 1982. *Meaningful to Behold:* View, Meditation and Action in Mahayana Buddhism, London, Wisdom Publications, 1980.

Rabten, Geshe, *Echoes of Voidness*, London, Wisdom Books. 1983.

Thubten Yeshe, Lama, and Zopa Rinpoche, *Wisdom Energy*, London, Wisdom Books, 1976.

Thubten Yeshe, Lama, *Introduction to Tantra*, compiled and edited by Jonathan Landaw, London, Wisdom Publications, 1987.

Blacking, John, *'A Commonsense View of Music'*, Cambridge, Cambridge University Press, 1987.

Boulding, Elise, *The Underside of History: A View of Women through Time*, Westview Press, Boulder, Colorado, 1976.

Capra, Fridjof, *The Tao of Physics*, London, Wildwood House, 1975. *The Turning Point:* Science, Society and the Rising Culture, London, Wildwood House, 1985.

Ferguson, Marilyn, *The Aquarian Conspiracy*, Los Angeles, Tarcher, 1980.

Gandhi, M.K. *An Autobiography or the Story of my Experiments with Truth*, Ahmadabad, Navajian Publishing House, 1927.

Hinde, Robert, Richard Leakey and 18 others, *Statement on Violence* (The Seville Declaration), Seville, Spain, May 16, 1976.

Johnston, William, *The Inner Eye of Love:* Mysticism and Religion, London, Collins, 1978

Jung, Carl Gustav, *Memories, Dreams and Reflections*, New York, Pantheon Books, 1961.

McAllister, Pam, *Reweaving the Web of Life:* Feminism and
  Nonviolence, Philadelphia, New Society Books, 1982.
Macy, Joanna, *Dharma and Development: Religion as Resource in the
  Sarvodya Self-help Movement,* Kumarian Press, 1983
Ouspensky, P.D. *In Search of the Miraculous,* London, Routledge
  and Kegan Paul, 1957. (This is the most comprehensive account
  of the teachings of G.I. Gurdjieff.)
Pagels, Elaine, *The Gnostic Gospels,* London, Weidenfeld and
  Nicholson, 1979.

Books in Print

RECOGNITION OF REALITY: REFLECTIONS AND PROSE POEMS
Adam Curle

Those of us living in the modern Western world (or 'North') have daily access to visual and factual images which travel with unprecedented rapidity from their place of origin to our newspaper page or television screen. Seemingly, these aim to 'inform' us about contemporary war, famine, poverty, summit meetings, human suffering, or other newsworthy events. How much of this we actually digest or comprehend is another matter. For many it is often enough to grapple with understanding our individual positions here and now, at this time, during this event or in this moment. And yet we are part of a wider world.

In **Recognition of Reality**, Adam Curle chooses not to lecture. This is a book of reflections; glimpses of inner and outer worlds caught in poetic form and always based on true experience. At times gentle, at times painful, these pieces combine to offer our Age a compassionate interpretation of reality, and vision for the future. **Recognition of Reality** seeks to convey the essential truth and spiritual essence so often distorted or unseen amid human suffering and despair. Only by coming to terms with our fundamental being will we succeed in transforming and renewing this earth.

ISBN : 869890 12 4 120pp Published 1987

Index

Orders

If you have difficulty ordering from a bookshop, you can order direct from Hawthorn Press, Bankfield House, 13 Wallbridge, Stroud, Glos GL5 3JA, UK.
Telephone: (0453) 757040
Fax: (0453) 753295